Art of the Knife

Joe Kertzman

©2007 Krause Publications

Published by

krause publications
An Imprint of F+W Publications

700 East State Street • Iola, WI 54990-0001
715-445-2214 • 888-457-2873
www.krausebooks.com

Our toll-free number to place an order or obtain
a free catalog is (800) 258-0929.

Library of Congress Control Number: 2006939723

ISBN-13: 978-0-89689-470-9
ISBN-10: 0-89689-470-3

Designed by Thomas Nelsen
Edited by Joe Kertzman

Printed in China

No Foreword . . .

No Introduction . . .

. . . Just Inspiration

The book has no introduction. So too does it lack a foreword written by an expert in the knife industry who has meaningful things to say about people who should be acknowledged, thanked or attributed for their contributions to the art of fashioning fine, handmade knives.

Such introductions and forewords are meaningful and welcome, often beautiful beginnings to books that readers delve into with gusto, soaking in the words like dry sponges on slick surfaces. Crediting those who act as unsung heroes, who create and contribute willingly, selflessly and without thought to credit or recognition is an admirable gesture. Far too often those who most deserve acknowledgement receive none.

There are icons in the custom knife industry—individuals who dedicated their lives to building functional, edged masterpieces that became treasured by collectors. Pillars of handmade knives exist who took man's oldest tool, the knife, to levels of artistry never before accomplished, seen or heretofore fathomed. There are men living stateside and abroad who basically built a market for handmade knives. They toiled in dust-choked, soot-filled knife shops, forging steel, shaping handles, engraving guards, scrimshawing ivory, etching blades, engineering springs, perfecting bolster shapes and finishing surface metal by hand, one fine grit at a time. They took the knives to shows, displayed their wares and waited respectfully while wide-eyed show goers ogled, felt, held and admired the knives, most unable to afford the cutlers' art.

Thank you to the predecessors of the modern custom knifemaker. For this we are indebted.

No, this isn't a book you delve into with gusto, hanging on every word and searching for deeper meaning. Nor is it a book you cuddle up with on a rainy day, afghan around your shoulders, coffee cup cradled in one hand and lamp turned low, as engrossing as a good novel and more fun to read than a teenage love letter.

This is an art knife book. There aren't many others like it in the world. It is rather an oddity. It acknowledges the contributions of only those whose knives are featured on and within its covers. In return, it also makes no excuses for the art form chosen. It requires no interaction.

The color is tremendous, the photography beautiful, the pages enlivened by jaw-dropping, finely crafted knives, those with edges so sweet their taste is mysterious. The carving, etching, engraving, gold inlaying, jewelling, stippling and sculpting are admirable and magical.

The way the knives are made is the essential ingredient. It is the beginning, the middle and the end of a story. The work speaks for itself. It acts as the introduction to the text, the foreword, the inspiration.

The author acknowledges this, the inspiring work of the knifemaker.

CONTENTS

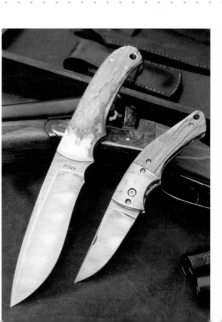

JEWELED AND INLAID ART KNIVES

Harumi Hirayama describes her Dragon Folding Fighter by saying, *"The dragon catches the pearl."* The knife is the second in a series made for Maj. Louis Chow, a serious collector of fighters. The first Dragon Fighter, fashioned in 1998, showcased a gold-lip-pearl dragon attempting to *"get the pearl."* Eight years later, the rainbow-white dragon has *"got the pearl."* The dragon is cut out of a whole, beautiful, large piece of mother-of-pearl using a 0/8 fine jeweler's saw blade. The knife features a hand-filed 440C blade, silver cloud-like bolsters, 18k-gold pins, a kaki-wood handle, silver claws and fangs, and 24k-gold lightning.
(Tomo Hasegawa photos)

Working with one of
Japan's finest knifemakers—
HARUMI HIRAYAMA—is an
experience to treasure. Hirayama's first
knife event was the 1985 Knifemakers' Guild Show
in Kansas City. She has been making knives since then and
says she enjoys "meeting her next knife." She made her first
edged creation, and they are edged creations, at the Tama Art
University. Now she attends the Guild Show every three or
four years, and the yearly Solvang Custom Knife Show.

She makes series of knives, often special orders from
collectors, and delivery time is three to six years. However,
while customers wait, Hirayama enjoys exchanging letters
with them, consulting on design. "Those are the happiest times
for me," she says. "I hope each of my knives will be carried by
generations to come."

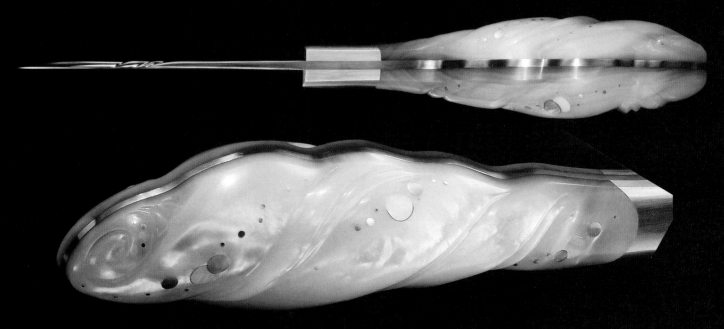

Harumi Hirayama's "Maelstrom" letter opener allows the lucky knife collector to grip a big water flow of mother-of-pearl. The handle material was cut from near the hinge of a large, whole mother-of-pearl shell, and then hand carved. Secondary, but not second fiddle, are the exquisite 440C blade, the silver bolsters and 18k-gold pins. Handle inlays include green snail, Japanese abalone, fresh-water pearl, gold and silver. (Tomo Hasegawa photos)

E. Jay Hendrickson is one of the American Bladesmith Society (ABS) members instrumental in the planning and formulation of the W.F. Moran School of Bladesmithing in Washington, Ark. He taught the basic "Introduction to Bladesmithing" course from 1989 through 2001, and he even wrote and illustrated the Introduction to Bladesmithing textbook that is presently used in the two-week training program.

"I currently serve on the ABS board of directors," Jay notes, "having been elected in 1986 and serving continuously since then. I took an early retirement from IBM in 1987 to become a full-time knifemaker."

Sprouting from the Masur-birch handle of E. Jay Hendrickson's Green River Skinner are fine silver wire vine-like inlays and an engraved nickel silver dogwood flower escutcheon. The bolster is file-worked nickel silver, and the 5160 blade slips seamlessly into a kudu sheath with basswood lining and a nickel silver throat. **(PointSeven** photo)

A few people contributed to Lee Gene Baskett's high-art folder, including George Fox who forged the damascus blade, Harry Limings who inlaid the gold in such a winning and wispy manner, and Baskett, himself, who carved the pearl, inlaid the gold thumb stud with a diamond, anodized the titanium liners blue, file worked the back spacer and inset more precious stones, including rubies, into the spine of the knife. **(PointSeven photo)**

The combination of silver wire inlay and scalloping of a curly maple handle enlivens an E. Jay Hendrickson D-guard bowie. Ten-and-three-eighths inches of damascus blade can barely compete with the scalloping, scrolls and decorative center handle inlay. **(PointSeven photo)**

The handle of Howard Hitchmough's locking-liner folder is high-contrast nickel damascus inlaid with 24k gold and then hot blued. More gold graces the pivot and thumb stud. A Damasteel blade and rope file-work along the handle spacer complete the piece.

The Peter Martin switchblade is one praying mantis you want on your side. The abalone and amber eyes stare straight into the powdered-mosaic-damascus blade, all of which is held up by an abalone and mammoth-tooth body and 14k-gold legs (the stand).

Is it the ruby and gold eyes or the 14k-gold horns of Peter Martin's "Rhinoceros Beetle" that make you buggy? The switchblade also sports a powdered-mosaic-damascus blade and bolsters, an antique-tortoise-shell back and an oosic belly.

"The Fire Within" art knife by Thomas Haslinger showcases a bright green and pink ammonite inlay within the boundaries of a mammoth-ivory handle. The Chris Marks damascus blade and bolsters add quite a bit of patterning to the pretty piece. Haslinger carved a large rhombic texture into the grip, breaking up the flat area of the handle material and giving it better purchase. The thumb stud and bail are 14k gold. **(T. Haslinger/Zannantonio photo)**

Designed after a symbolic bald eagle of the Haida tribe, Thomas Haslinger's fixed blade features a beak-looking BG-42 blade inlaid with black onyx (the eagle eye), gold and diamond (the latter two making up the pupil). The artist inlayed gold circles into the ironwood bolsters, representing the circle of life, and carved the mother-of-pearl handle into a wing-like pattern. **(G. Poetzel and T. Haslinger photo)**

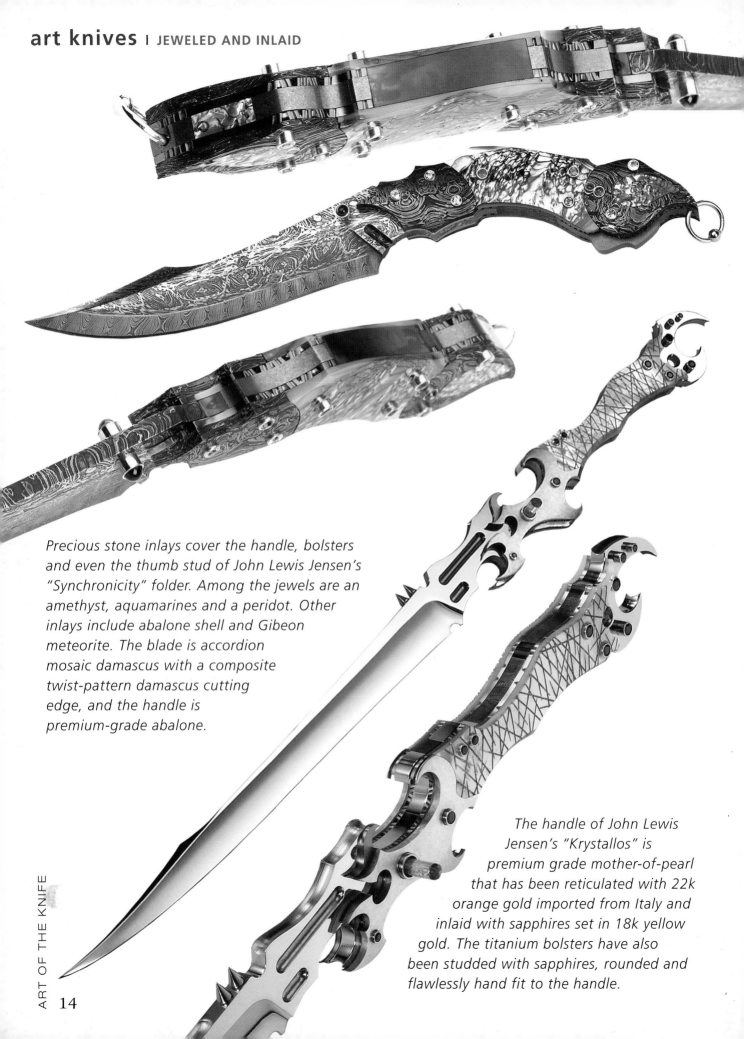

Precious stone inlays cover the handle, bolsters and even the thumb stud of John Lewis Jensen's "Synchronicity" folder. Among the jewels are an amethyst, aquamarines and a peridot. Other inlays include abalone shell and Gibeon meteorite. The blade is accordion mosaic damascus with a composite twist-pattern damascus cutting edge, and the handle is premium-grade abalone.

The handle of John Lewis Jensen's "Krystallos" is premium grade mother-of-pearl that has been reticulated with 22k orange gold imported from Italy and inlaid with sapphires set in 18k yellow gold. The titanium bolsters have also been studded with sapphires, rounded and flawlessly hand fit to the handle.

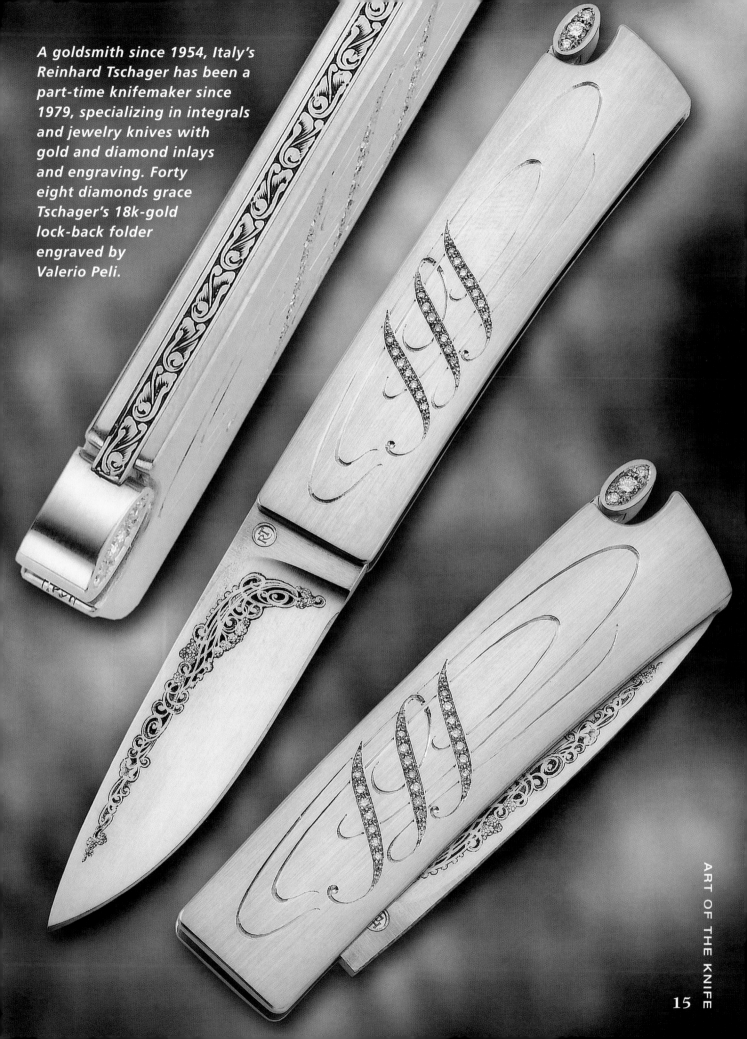

A goldsmith since 1954, Italy's Reinhard Tschager has been a part-time knifemaker since 1979, specializing in integrals and jewelry knives with gold and diamond inlays and engraving. Forty eight diamonds grace Tschager's 18k-gold lock-back folder engraved by Valerio Peli.

Gold pins and diamonds dot the black-palm handle of Reinhard Tschager's integral ATS-34 "City Knife." The piece trails a gold chain and pendant behind it.

Seven carats of fine diamonds and 57.5 carats of green tourmaline grace the hilt and furniture of Jot Singh Khalsa's incredible sword. Many people collaborated on the piece, including Devin Thomas who provided the ladder-pattern damascus, Tim Adlam and his 24k-gold inlay and engraving, Vince Evans with the scabbard fabrication, and Julie Warenski who applied the gemstone setting. The ocean-jasper hilt features heavy gold/zirconium plating over sterling silver.

(PointSeven photo)

Silver-wire-inlaid flowers, stems and leaves enliven the tiger-maple tsuka (handle) and saya (sheath) of Fred Ott's Japanese-style tanto. It also sports an 11-inch, 1084-15N20-and-L-6 damascus blade, a copper habaki (blade collar) and buffalo-horn tips at the ends of the tsuka and saya.

(Hoffman photo)

ART OF THE KNIFE

17

The Skilled Art of Scrimshaw

CURT ERICKSON UTAH

It would be a dirty shame to slip the Curt Erickson boot knife into a boot, and thus cover up the scrimshawed elephant-ivory handle. Scrimshaw artist John Stahl forever immortalized a snowy owl and mother polar bear and cub within the pores of the ivory. The light blue sky and shades of blue snow do wonders for the "wow factor" of the fancy fixed blade with engraved bolsters.
(PointSeven photo)

While one Siberian tiger busies itself bothering a wren, a mother tiger and cubs lie in waiting. The Fred Carter hunting knife is all the better for the color scrimshaw from the hands of skilled artist John Stahl. John says the winter wren is the only wren to be found in the Old World and on all continents in the Northern hemisphere. (PointSeven photo)

John Stahl captured the character of a curious raccoon through "pin and ink," or scrimshawed drawings of the critter on the elephant-ivory handle of a W.R. Carnes folder. (SharpByCoop.com photo)

Tom Ferry's Joan of Arc dagger is defined not only by an intricately scrimshawed ivory handle, but also by a mosaic-damascus blade exhibiting crosses, spades and other shapes. The guard and pommel are also damascus.
(Mitch Lum photo)

A talented scrimshaw artist, Sandra Brady depicted 11 wildcats in a collage setting on the ivory handle of a Don Lozier dagger. The natural expressions of the cats, including intense hunting gazes and predatory growls of a couple cats, capture their tension-filled energies, which are contrasted by the seemingly benign expressions of the others. Each minute whisker and hair seems ready to come to life.

Lozier's dagger also features a Jerry Rados ladder-pattern damascus blade, and a nickel silver guard and pommel showcasing the engraving and gold-inlaying talent of Julie Warenski.

(Weyer of Toledo photo)

SANDRA BRADY, at the tender age of 16, began to learn the precise and exacting artistry of scrimshaw. After school and on weekends, Sandra worked as a scrimshaw artist for a local burgeoning jewelry company. After a year, she decided to go out on her own and toured northern Ohio, selling scrimshaw at craft exhibitions and gun shows.

Brady is versed in many artistic media, such as drawing, printmaking, oil painting and pastels. She majored in art at the University of Toledo with a particular focus on anatomy and the human form.

"My true artistic passion will always be scrimshaw," she says. "My particular strong point is scrimming wildlife scenes."

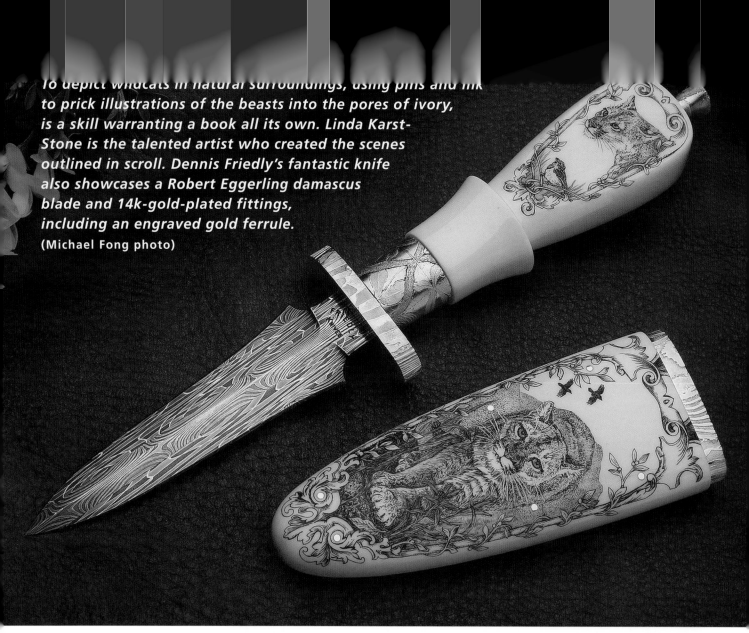

To depict wildcats in natural surroundings, using pins and ink to prick illustrations of the beasts into the pores of ivory, is a skill warranting a book all its own. Linda Karst-Stone is the talented artist who created the scenes outlined in scroll. Dennis Friedly's fantastic knife also showcases a Robert Eggerling damascus blade and 14k-gold-plated fittings, including an engraved gold ferrule. (Michael Fong photo)

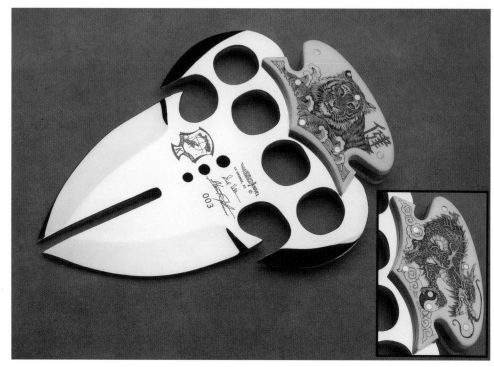

Linda Karst-Stone's colorful scrimshaw of a tiger and dragon enlivens a Gil Hibben "Kenpo Fist" fantasy knife. Kenpo, otherwise known as kempo, is a common Japanese term for martial arts that is the translation of the Chinese quánf meaning "fist principles," "way of the fist" or "law of the fist form." (Michael Fong photo)

Gary "Garbo" Williams scrimshawed a stoic, handsome Native American in full headdress on the ivory handle of a Gene Baskett folder. The knife sports a Colt .45 pistol grip, a 440C blade, blue-anodized-titanium liners and a ruby-inlaid gold thumb stud. (PointSeven photo)

"I have always been interested in art and got a degree in art education at Eastern Kentucky University," says GARY "GARBO" WILLIAMS. "I have worked as an illustrator for the U.S. Army since 1976, and in that time I have also pursued other freelance jobs, including sculpting ceramic, creating limited edition prints and various illustration work.

"I have illustrated for books, magazines, calendars and record labels, and have done fine art prints. It was through the circulation of the prints that I was introduced to scrimshaw," Gary explains. "A custom knifemaker named Gene Baskett liked my paintings and contacted me with the idea of scrimshaw work on his knives. That was in 1987 and I have been primarily involved in this medium since that time. It seems, through scrimshaw, I found my niche in the art world and gained a very good friend in Gene."

Top left: Gene Baskett's "Buffalo Skinner" parades a fossil-walrus-ivory handle scrimshawed by Gary "Garbo" Williams with the image of a buffalo in color as big as the plains where the beast roamed. A stippled-brass guard and file-worked 440C blade make it all the knife a Westerner needs. (PointSeven photo)

Left: The Northwest is illustrated in art and human form on the fossil-walrus-ivory handle of a Gene Baskett knife, thanks to the Gary "Garbo" Williams scrimshaw, as well as the Harry Limings engraving across a brass finger guard. Robert Eggerling contributed the damascus blade to complete the package. (PointSeven photo)

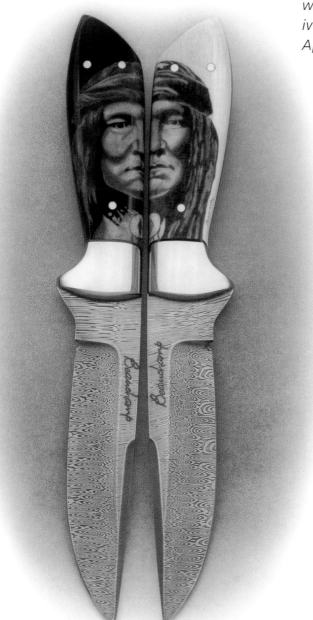

Left: It took twin damascus fixed blades, one with a water-buffalo-horn handle, and one with a mammoth-ivory grip, for Gaetan Beauchamp to fully illustrate the Apache chief Chato. **(Alain Miville-Deschenes photo)**

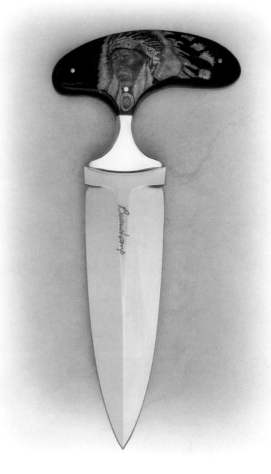

Above: So realistic is the Indian chief that it's impossible to believe Gaetan Beauchamp used needles and ink to create the proud warrior's image on the water-buffalo-horn handle of a 9-inch push dagger. **(Alain Miville-Deschenes photo)**

The rugged and breathtaking terrain of northern Quebec is home to some of the most majestic and spectacular wildlife North America has to offer. It is also home to one of the most prolific and talented artists that Canada has to offer—GAETAN BEAUCHAMP.

"Those familiar with his exquisite scrimshaw can attest to the realism and the lifelike qualities of the reverse method [white ink on dark surfaces, the latter including buffalo horn and other black backgrounds] that Beauchamp has popularized," knife collector Del Corsi says.

"Wildlife is indeed Beauchamp's specialty," Corsi adds. "It continually amazes me each time I view animals that he has portrayed. His style seems to bring the animals to life. It is simply amazing."

Gaetan Beauchamp "reverse scrimshawed" the black-buffalo-horn handle of Bob Patrick's Ralph Bone-style bowie in an Indian motif. The knife sports an ATS-34 blade, a mokumé guard, mammoth-ivory spacers and a buffalo-horn pommel. **(Gallagher photo)**

Collaboration was the key to the large damascus bowie, but knifemaker Herman Schneider can be credited for pulling it all together. The sexy scrimshaw is by Darrel Morris, the steel lion head from the hands of engraver Ron Skaggs, and the gold work by embellisher Julie Warenski. (Hiro Soga photo)

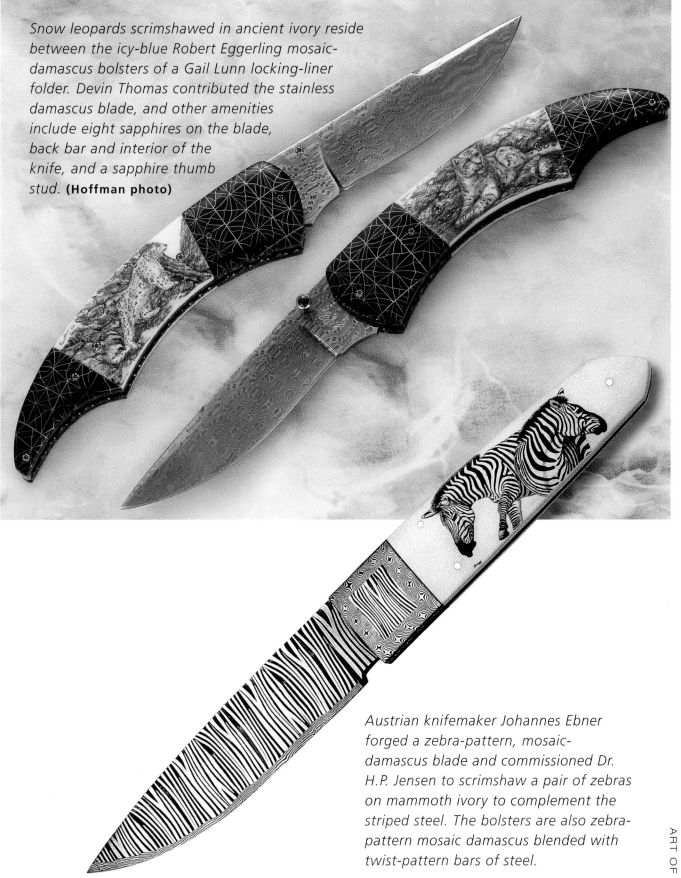

Snow leopards scrimshawed in ancient ivory reside between the icy-blue Robert Eggerling mosaic-damascus bolsters of a Gail Lunn locking-liner folder. Devin Thomas contributed the stainless damascus blade, and other amenities include eight sapphires on the blade, back bar and interior of the knife, and a sapphire thumb stud. **(Hoffman photo)**

Austrian knifemaker Johannes Ebner forged a zebra-pattern, mosaic-damascus blade and commissioned Dr. H.P. Jensen to scrimshaw a pair of zebras on mammoth ivory to complement the striped steel. The bolsters are also zebra-pattern mosaic damascus blended with twist-pattern bars of steel.

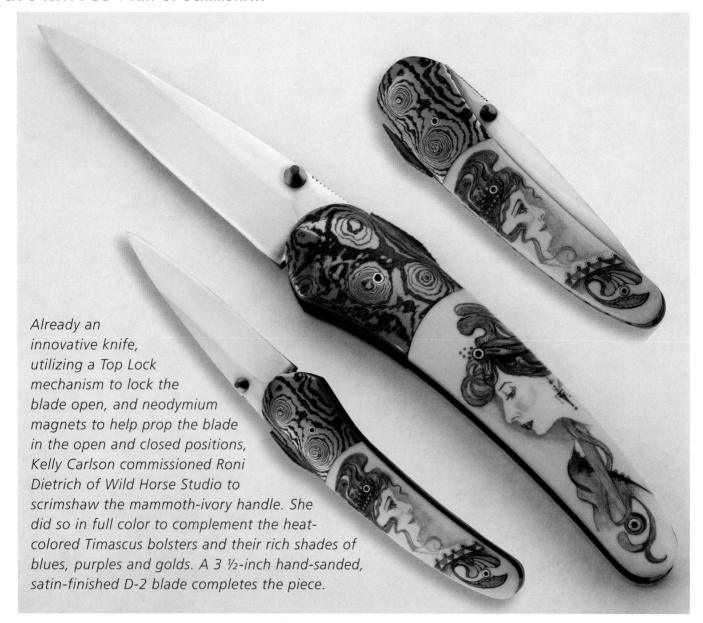

Already an innovative knife, utilizing a Top Lock mechanism to lock the blade open, and neodymium magnets to help prop the blade in the open and closed positions, Kelly Carlson commissioned Roni Dietrich of Wild Horse Studio to scrimshaw the mammoth-ivory handle. She did so in full color to complement the heat-colored Timascus bolsters and their rich shades of blues, purples and golds. A 3 ½-inch hand-sanded, satin-finished D-2 blade completes the piece.

"Over the past few years, in addition to developing my own assisted-opening mechanism for folders, I've also invented a new gadget for one of the oldest folding-knife actions—the slip joint," explains KELLY CARLSON. "Instead of a heavy spring to hold the blade open and closed, my patent-pending system utilizes strong neodymium magnets to securely prop the blade open and closed.

"The benefit of this method," Carlson continues, "is that the opening and closing resistance is substantially reduced, and no resistance is applied to the blade while traveling to its respective open or closed positions, resulting in a light, smooth action that can be easily operated with one hand. Traditional slip-joint mechanisms typically require two strong hands to operate."

Last winter, Carlson extended the concept to his Top Lock mechanism, which utilizes a spring-loaded bolt to securely lock a blade into the open position, and the neodymium magnet to hold it securely, but lightly, in a closed position.

Scrimshaw of a tiger's eyes embellishes the tiger-bone handle of a Vladimir Pulis mosaic-damascus masterpiece, one that can be slipped seamlessly into the leather and snakeskin sheath. **(Ivan Cillik photo)**

At top is a Vladimir Pulis knife in a linear-damascus blade, mokumé spacers and a water-buffalo-horn handle, the latter scrimshawed in the likeness of the beast from which the bone came. Beneath that knife comes a stupendous mosaic-damascus cutter with images of a howling wolf visible within the tile-like squares of pattern-welded steel. It also features mokumé spacers but substitutes walrus tusk for the buffalo horn of the first knife grip. **(Ivan Cillik photo)**

Vladimir Pulis's "First Sin" knife is embellished with beautiful scrimshaw in an Adam and Eve Biblical motif, including a snake, apple tree and love scene. The knife also showcases a silver, snakewood and ostrich bone handle, a mosaic-damascus blade and a bull-bone sheath with a snakeskin upper. (Ivan Cillik photos)

The wizardry of the damascus dagger is further emphasized by the bearded gent scrimshawed in color on the ivory handle. The dagger also displays a carved and textured stainless steel guard and pommel, and sterling silver braided bands.

In undertaking knifemaking as a career, JOT SINGH KHALSA sought out established knifemakers and bladesmiths throughout the United States from whom to learn about grinding and forging, the best steels and their heat treatment, and information on knife and sword construction and fabrication. "I quickly developed the necessary skills and experience to become a member of the Knifemakers' Guild," he says, "and have enjoyed making knives and swords full time since 1978.

"I also serve as a Sikh minister. As far as I know, I'm the only Sikh member of the Knifemakers' Guild. I'm easy to find at knife shows as 'the guy in white, wearing a turban,'" Khalsa relates. "Luckily for me, colleagues and customers know that I'm one of the good guys!"

Francesco Pachi had an advantage over other knifemakers—having a close relationship with a gal named Mirella Pachi who scrimshawed the African "big five" (lion, tiger, rhino, elephant and water buffalo) on his knife handle. Francesco added a bit of fancy file work of his own along the blade spine. **(Pachi photo)**

In the beginning, crafting knives was but yet another hobby for **LEON TREIBER**, a Texan with many diverse interests. He became skilled in the art quickly, and by 1991, it became obvious that his passion for making knives was more than a passing interest. His focus grew more intense as he dedicated himself to creating what are widely recognized today as his trademark folding knives.

Treiber's push for perfection drives him to constantly create ambitious, fresh knife designs, each one beautifully unique, but every one bearing his distinct signature and fine touches.

Right: Linda Karst Stone can be credited for scrimshawing the lifelike cougar and bird of prey onto the elephant-ivory handle of Leon Treiber's lock-back folding knife, and A.E. Scott is responsible for the engraving on the finger guard.

The orange of the tiger, that Linda Karst Stone scrimshawed especially for a Leon Treiber auto folder, is mimicked in the mokumé bolsters. Mammoth ivory surrounds the tiger that is, in turn, scrimshawed on elephant ivory. Devin Thomas delivered the stainless damascus blade material.

THE HIGH ART OF ENGRAVED BLADES

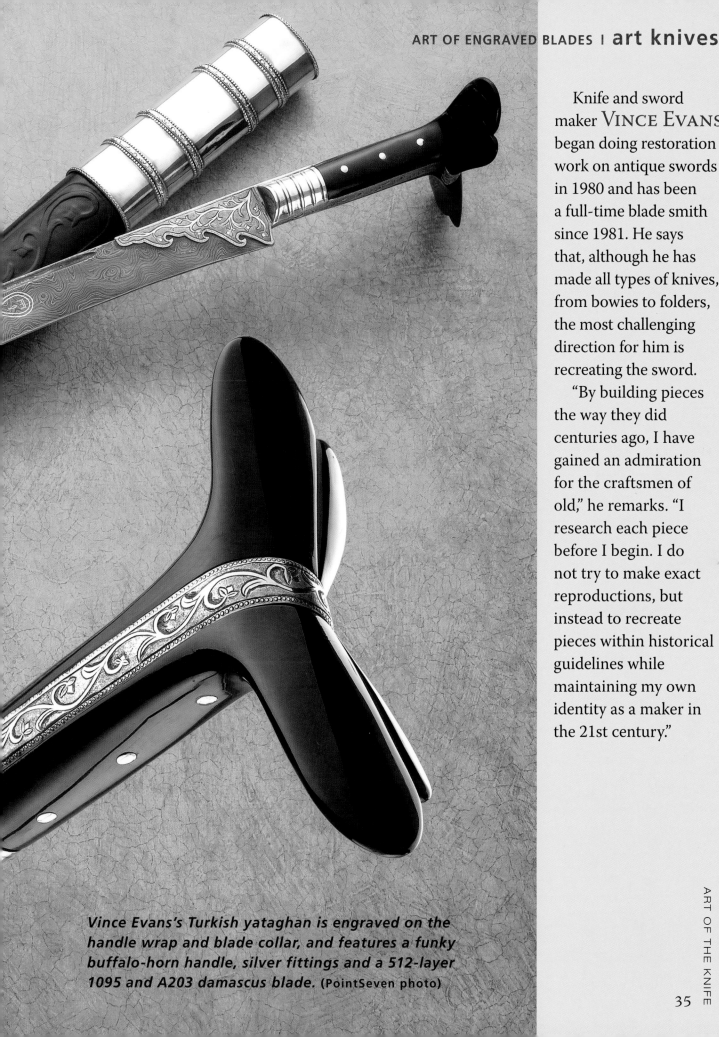

Knife and sword maker VINCE EVANS began doing restoration work on antique swords in 1980 and has been a full-time blade smith since 1981. He says that, although he has made all types of knives, from bowies to folders, the most challenging direction for him is recreating the sword.

"By building pieces the way they did centuries ago, I have gained an admiration for the craftsmen of old," he remarks. "I research each piece before I begin. I do not try to make exact reproductions, but instead to recreate pieces within historical guidelines while maintaining my own identity as a maker in the 21st century."

Vince Evans's Turkish yataghan is engraved on the handle wrap and blade collar, and features a funky buffalo-horn handle, silver fittings and a 512-layer 1095 and A203 damascus blade. (PointSeven photo)

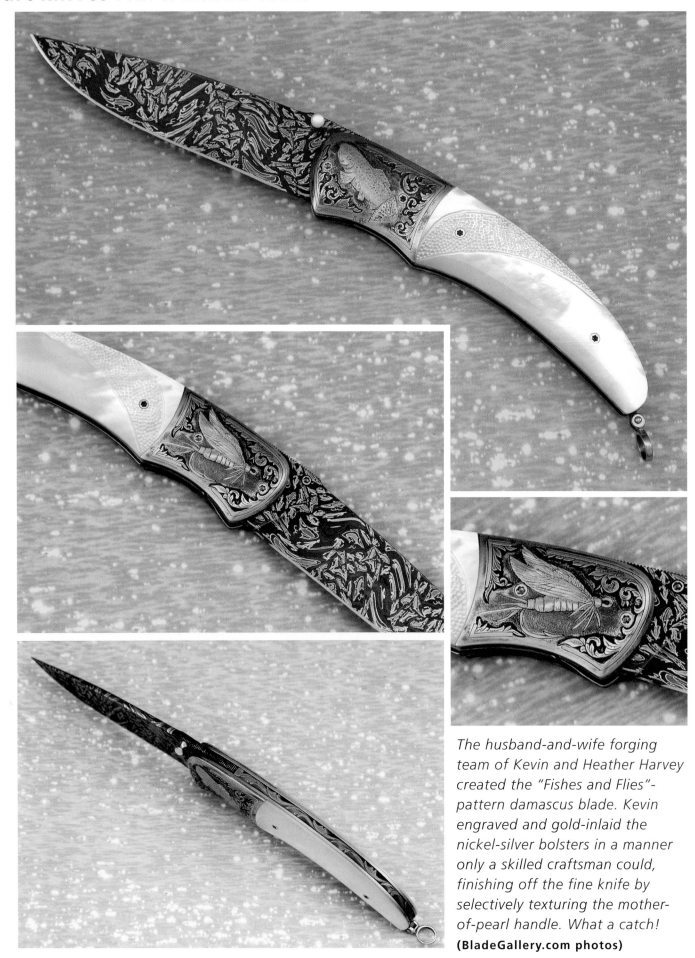

The husband-and-wife forging team of Kevin and Heather Harvey created the "Fishes and Flies"-pattern damascus blade. Kevin engraved and gold-inlaid the nickel-silver bolsters in a manner only a skilled craftsman could, finishing off the fine knife by selectively texturing the mother-of-pearl handle. What a catch!

(BladeGallery.com photos)

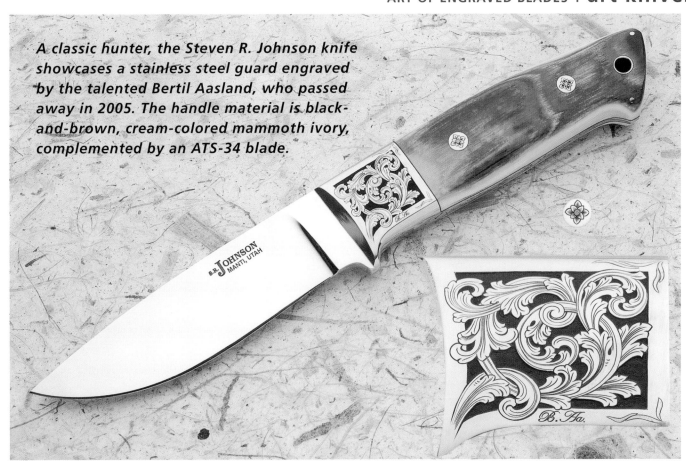

A classic hunter, the Steven R. Johnson knife showcases a stainless steel guard engraved by the talented Bertil Aasland, who passed away in 2005. The handle material is black-and-brown, cream-colored mammoth ivory, complemented by an ATS-34 blade.

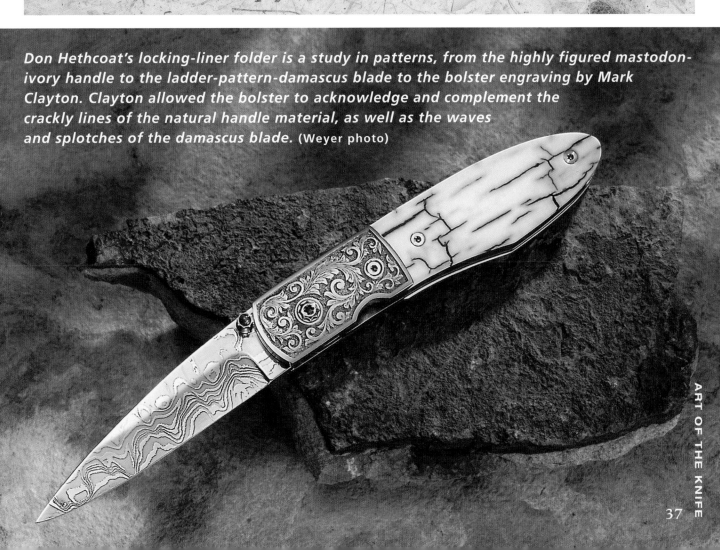

Don Hethcoat's locking-liner folder is a study in patterns, from the highly figured mastodon-ivory handle to the ladder-pattern-damascus blade to the bolster engraving by Mark Clayton. Clayton allowed the bolster to acknowledge and complement the crackly lines of the natural handle material, as well as the waves and splotches of the damascus blade. (Weyer photo)

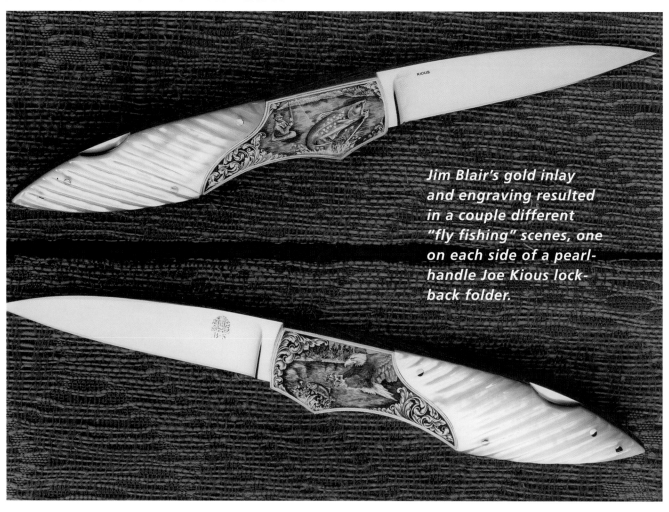

Jim Blair's gold inlay and engraving resulted in a couple different "fly fishing" scenes, one on each side of a pearl-handle Joe Kious lock-back folder.

The work of engraver JIM BLAIR consists primarily of game scenes in Bulino style, semi-relief engraving and deep relief engravings. He creates inlays using precious metals or other suitable materials. Wild-game engravings can be recreated in steel from full, detailed scenes, or from a print of an animal head alone. Each scene is created individually to suit the client's taste.

Blair works in English, rose, Arabesque, Victorian, floral and German scrolls, but ultimately he designs custom scroll to fit each individual piece.

Far left & right: *As Jim Blair worked his engraving tools on the stainless steel handle of a Kirk Rexroat damascus folder, water began washing over the exposed bodies of nature lovers, one on each side of the exquisite piece.*

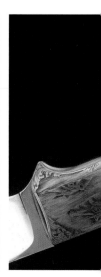

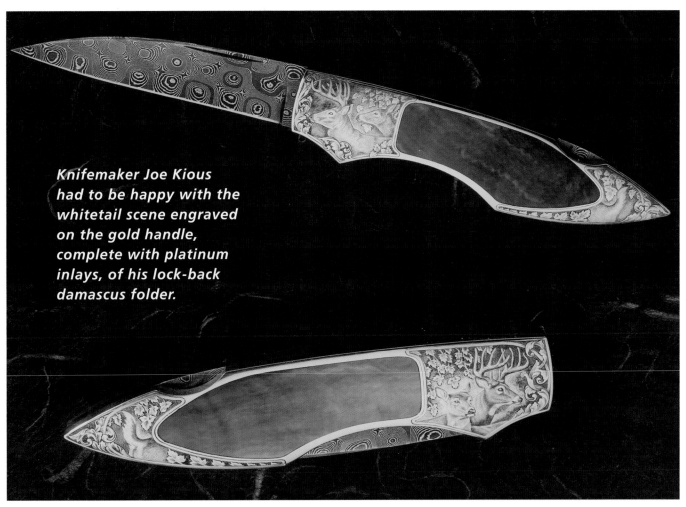

Knifemaker Joe Kious had to be happy with the whitetail scene engraved on the gold handle, complete with platinum inlays, of his lock-back damascus folder.

He learned his craft in classes at the National Rifle Association School in Trinidad, Col. The balance of his technique and artistic style were of his own development, and he prefers to work on custom guns and knives using time-tested, traditional tools. The tools include a burin, chisel and hammer, and super-fine detail is attained through the use of a microscope.

Below middle: *Brad Zinker built a knife with a hippo-tooth handle scrimshawed in an underwater plant life scene, and Jim Blair completed the hippo/water theme by engraving wading hippos on the knife bolster.*

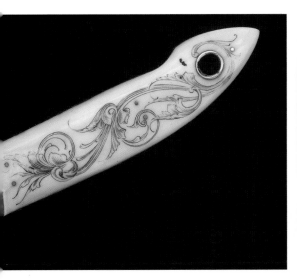

The harmonic designs of Argentina knifemaker PEDRO GIBERT often exhibit engraving that complements the blade, guard, bolster and handle material. "Finely finished, my pieces can be viewed as real jewels, without losing sight of their intended use, because they are tools to be employed in the most exigent jobs," Pedro says.

Left & below: *The guard and pommel of Pedro Gibert's integral fixed blade were engraved with a burin. The craftsman outfitted the knife with an Austrian steel blade, a snakewood handle and a tanned leather sheath embroidered with cotton yarn.*

He keeps a register for customers with drawings of each knife he makes, including the technical specifications, place of manufacture (hand manufacture) and date. All knives are fashioned from hardened and tempered Austrian steel, which generations of craftsmen make in a special oven with a digital pyrometer, thus guaranteeing the perfect heat treatment.

***Right & below:** Engraving along the blade tang and spine of Pedro Gibert's art knife give it a formal, elegant feel. The stag handle completes the package, and the leather sheath is an added bonus.*

Right: *Knifemaker Tim Herman's name and the art of color engraving have become synonymous. To complement a brilliant Austrian opal handle inlay, Herman engraved the 416 stainless steel frame in an Australian wildlife theme. The knife features a kangaroo on one side and a koala bear on the other.* **(Michael P. Artemis photo)**

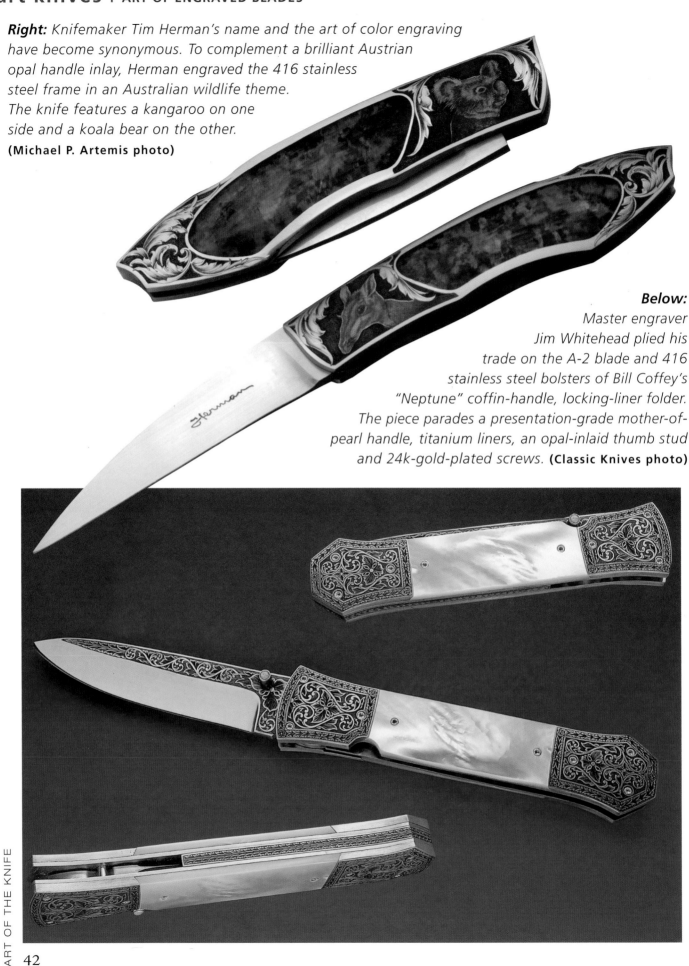

Below:
Master engraver Jim Whitehead plied his trade on the A-2 blade and 416 stainless steel bolsters of Bill Coffey's "Neptune" coffin-handle, locking-liner folder. The piece parades a presentation-grade mother-of-pearl handle, titanium liners, an opal-inlaid thumb stud and 24k-gold-plated screws. **(Classic Knives photo)**

When T.R. Overeynder gets on a roll fashioning folding daggers, they start coming out in pairs. The blades and 416 stainless steel frames are shaped identically, but the similarities stop there. Blades include Mike Norris "Crazy Lace" damascus and 154CM, and handle inlays are black-lip pearl and white mother-of-pearl. Two golden boys of engraving, Ray Cover Jr. and Ron Skaggs, respectively, engraved the demonic knife (left) and the skull-and-vixen scene at right. **(PointSeven photo)**

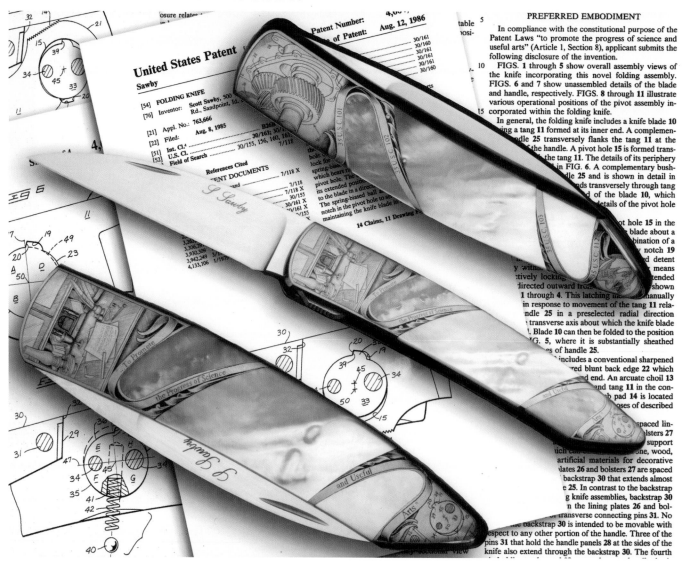

Above: *Scott Sawby's stainless steel folder was engraved in Bulino style by Ray Cover Jr. On either side and between mother-of-pearl handle inlays are patents that promote the progress of science, including a vintage desk where a patent attorney would prepare an application; a patent figure illustrating the actual locking mechanism of the knife; a patent figure of another mechanical device; a ribbon listing various patent statutes; a ribbon with a quote from the U.S. Constitution; and the United States Patent and Trademark Office seal.* (**Michael P. Artemis photo**)

Dwight Towell is one of only a few who can change a folding boot knife into high art, in this case through the engraving of a stainless steel handle frame, gold beading around a jade handle inlay and more engraved scrolls pointing toward the tip of the edged steel.

© *Michael Fong Photography '06*

Knifemaker and master engraver Jim Sornberger outdid himself in fashioning a fully engraved San Francisco art dagger. Among the goodies are California gold-quartz handle inlays, a 14k-gold handle frame and guard, a coin-silver and 14k-gold sheath (also fully engraved), and a 5 ½-inch ATS-34 blade. The size 18 pocket watch features four-color, gold engraving by the maker.
(Michael Fong photos)

Stan Fujisaka and Jim Sornberger teamed up to create a colossally engraved locking-liner folder. The spunky, rose-color, gold-quartz handle inlay is surrounded by engraved titanium depicting an eagle, a crest, flowers, a knight and a bear, among other strong visuals.

Various colors of gold quartz, California jade and cinnabar mining ore samples under mineral glass add brilliant splashes to Jim Sornberger's California dress knife. The 14k-gold handle and sheath are embellished with Jim's masterful engraving. (Hoffman photo)

Right: Ross Mitsuyuki drew the dragon freehand before engraving it on the titanium handle of his frame-lock folder. The handle was then anodized different colors. Paul Bos heat-treated the 440C blade.

Opposite page: Folding knives are Matthew Lerch's love, and his work encompasses anything from tactical folders to high-end art pieces, the latter of which includes the Richfield Double Action Liner Lock engraved by Ray Cover Jr.

On one side of the handle, a swan wraps itself around the naked body of the fairer sex, while on the other side a burly man is enveloped by a bird of prey. The handle inlay is black-lip pearl, and the damascus is a Turkish Twist pattern complements of Jerry Rados. Other features include 18k-gold inlays, a fluted thumb stud and fancy file work.

Wayne Hensley's flat-ground, satin-finished ATS-34 fixed blade was royally treated to bolster engraving by none other than Jim Small, who book-ended a mother-of-pearl handle with his artwork, and even decorated the head of the handle pin. **(Hoffman photo)**

"I love my job and especially the wonderful people I meet," says Joe Kious, who has been making knives since 1969. He was a teacher, fashioning knives on evenings and weekends, until 1980 when he went into full-time knifemaking. "That was 27 years ago now," he proudly announces.

Kious's Model 6 inter-frame folder shows much plumage in the way of parrots ruffling their feathers on the steel handle of his folding dagger. Ray Cover Jr. is credited for the colorful, feathery engraving, and the knife is built with an ATS-34 blade and a black-lip-pearl handle inlay. **(SharpByCoop.com photo)**

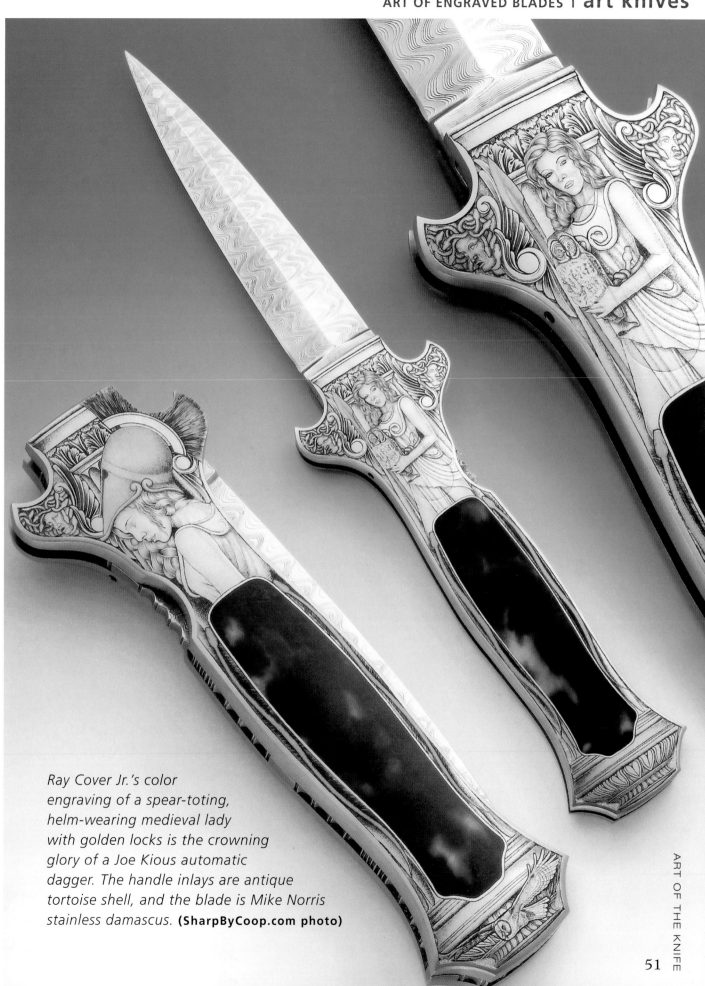

Ray Cover Jr.'s color engraving of a spear-toting, helm-wearing medieval lady with golden locks is the crowning glory of a Joe Kious automatic dagger. The handle inlays are antique tortoise shell, and the blade is Mike Norris stainless damascus. **(SharpByCoop.com photo)**

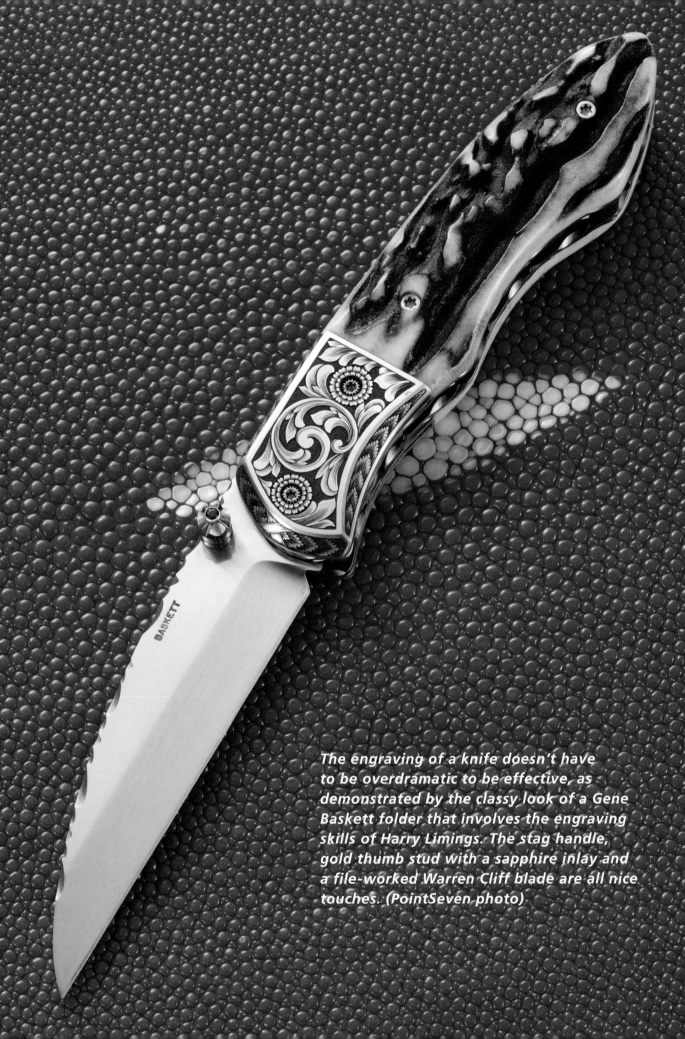

The engraving of a knife doesn't have to be overdramatic to be effective, as demonstrated by the classy look of a Gene Baskett folder that involves the engraving skills of Harry Limings. The stag handle, gold thumb stud with a sapphire inlay and a file-worked Warren Cliff blade are all nice touches. (PointSeven photo)

Al Scott engraved the stainless-steel and gold bolsters of a Leon Treiber folder. Inlaid into the Texas ebony handle of the ATS-34 knife are a sterling-silver badge and Texas Paterson Colt five-shooter. Vine file work along the blade spine is an added touch.

A member of the Knifemakers' Guild since 1995, and a voting member of the Guild since 1997, LEON TREIBER takes to the road at least five times a year to exhibit his knives in shows across the nation. *BLADE Magazine*®, *Knives Illustrated*, the *Knives* annual book and the *Points of Interest V* book by Jim Weyer have all featured Treiber's knives. Sportsmen and collectors alike appreciate and seek out his edged tools.

Whether a dragon or sea serpent, the engraved creature on the guard of Johannes Ebner's knife lashes out in protest of having to be the only evil being in such beautiful surroundings. The knife materials include a stunning mammoth-ivory grip with a roadmap of lines and blemishes, and a mosaic-damascus blade encompassed by a circulating bar of twist-pattern damascus. Armin Bundschuh is responsible for the enslaving engraving.

Armin Bundschuh's gold inlay and engraving enhances a shockingly beautiful Johannes Ebner knife that includes a blade with a mosaic-damascus core and twist-damascus outer layers. The handle of the piece is mammoth ivory.

Whether the lion engraved by Chris Meyer on the guard of Jot Singh Khalsa's folding kirpan is a protector of the weak or master of his own domain is up to interpretation. But one thing is for certain, the jasper-handle, locking-liner folder, complete with a nickel-damascus blade and black-pearl accents, is worthy of the king of any jungle, tribe or kingdom. **(PointSeven photo)**

"It wouldn't be a lie for me to say that knifemaking has been a spiritual experience for me," allows JOT SINGH KHALSA. "When I was 19 years old and in college studying fine arts [with a focus on gold and silver smithing], I began to practice Kundalini yoga and meditation. Through my affiliation with our non-sectarian yoga organization, the 3H0 Foundation, I met Yogi Bhajan, a spiritual master who was also a member of the Sikh religion.

"One of the symbols of the Sikh religion is the kirpan [knife], which is worn to remind one to be the protector of the weak and innocent," Khalsa explains. "The symbolic kirpans that friends were obtaining from India were and are still not of great quality. Encouragement from a couple of Sikh friends led me to acquire the special metal-smithing skills required for knifemaking."

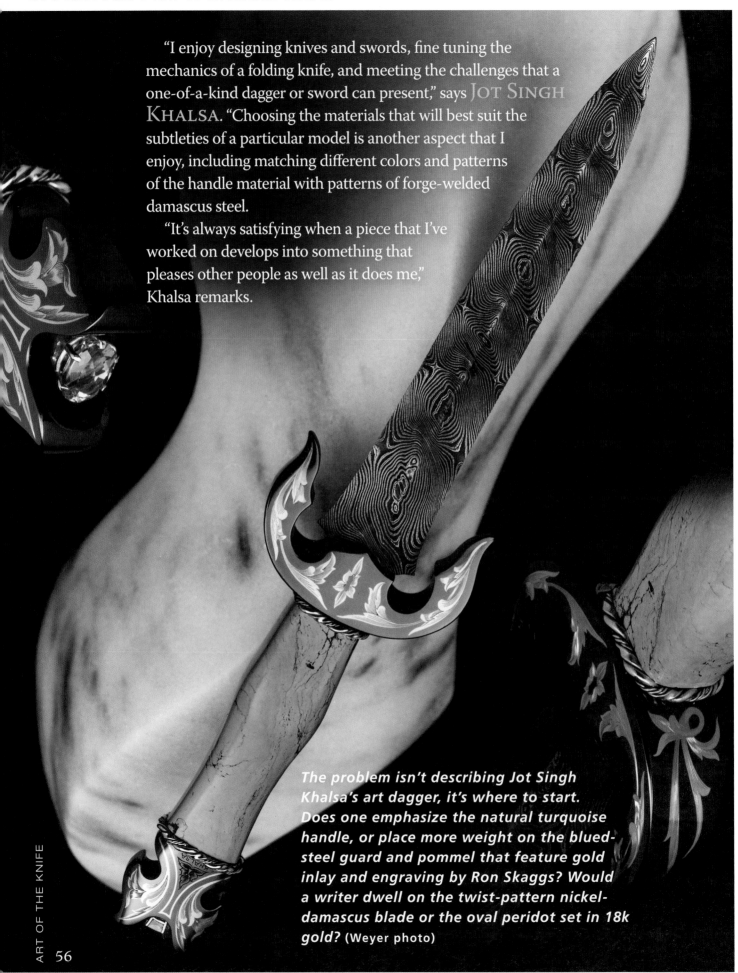

"I enjoy designing knives and swords, fine tuning the mechanics of a folding knife, and meeting the challenges that a one-of-a-kind dagger or sword can present," says JOT SINGH KHALSA. "Choosing the materials that will best suit the subtleties of a particular model is another aspect that I enjoy, including matching different colors and patterns of the handle material with patterns of forge-welded damascus steel.

"It's always satisfying when a piece that I've worked on develops into something that pleases other people as well as it does me," Khalsa remarks.

The problem isn't describing Jot Singh Khalsa's art dagger, it's where to start. Does one emphasize the natural turquoise handle, or place more weight on the blued-steel guard and pommel that feature gold inlay and engraving by Ron Skaggs? Would a writer dwell on the twist-pattern nickel-damascus blade or the oval peridot set in 18k gold? (Weyer photo)

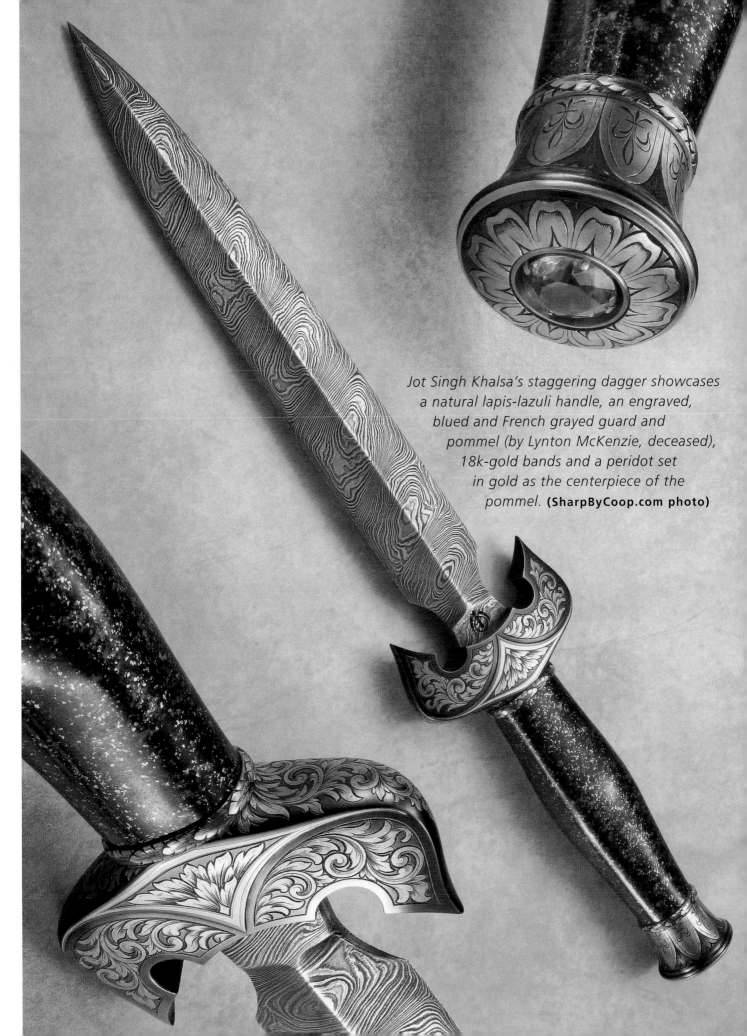

Jot Singh Khalsa's staggering dagger showcases a natural lapis-lazuli handle, an engraved, blued and French grayed guard and pommel (by Lynton McKenzie, deceased), 18k-gold bands and a peridot set in gold as the centerpiece of the pommel. **(SharpByCoop.com photo)**

Can a fixed blade be a pocketknife? Can a knife become jewelry? Does gold belong on gentleman's pocket cutlery? All questions receive a resounding "yes" after witnessing the beauty of Reinhard Tschager's pearl-handle jewel of a knife. The gold engraving is by the Italian engraver Valerio Peli.

(Francesco Pachi photo)

"My goal is to create one-of-a-kind knives that I hope will be considered family treasures to be passed on to future generations," says Howard Hitchmough. "Like most everyone, I had begun building fixed-blade hunting knives but soon discovered that I welcomed the challenge of folding knives. Their construction requires accurate fitting and proper mechanical functioning, as well as attention to aesthetic design."

Left: Attention to detail is apparent in every aspect of Howard Hitchmough's art knife, from the stainless steel bolsters engraved and gold inlaid by Tim George, to the mammoth-ivory handle, ladder-pattern-damascus blade and mauve-colored titanium liners.

Middle: Julie Warenski's engraving and gold inlay work highlight a Howard Hitchmough art folder and park themselves between a pleasant premium-grade, black-lip-pearl handle and a Devin Thomas damascus blade. More gold reveals itself in the form of the handle screws, bail and "dot openers."

Right: The stainless steel handle of a Howard Hitchmough folder is beautifully engraved and gold inlaid by Tim George, who also engraved the 18k-gold pivot collars. The piece showcases a 2 ½-inch Heimskringla-pattern Damasteel blade, anodized-titanium liners, a file-worked back spacer and an 18k-gold thumb stud set with a sapphire.

HOWARD HITCHMOUGH'S

philosophy is that modern knifemaking is a logical continuation of man's desire to build better tools. "Today we are fortunate to have an enormous range of materials exceptionally suitable for making knives," he says. "These, together with modern technology, enable us to create knives that were unimaginable only a few decades ago.

"Technique, alone, however, is not enough; a proper understanding of design is essential if one wants to make aesthetically pleasing knives," Hitchmough reasons. "I attempt to use all my skills and knowledge to produce beautiful knives that will survive far into the future."

Engraver Ron Skaggs executes an Art Deco theme through the use of 24k gold, 18k pink gold and fine silver on the handle of a Howard Hitchmough folding knife. The Damasteel damascus blade is equally worthy of recognition.

Opposite page: "My knives are as varied as the individuals who own them," JODY MULLER proposes. "One is big and bold and has a dramatic damascus pattern and unique, carved handle. Another may be a small folder with a delicate hand-engraved blade and slim ivory grip. Each is a one-of-a-kind piece that evolves within my imagination.

"Some knives begin as ideas, and others grow from pieces of damascus, or a slab of pearl or wood. Every knife I produce is my best knife," Muller insists. "The degree to which I enjoy my work is evident in all stages of knifemaking, from forging steel to adding my Muller 'JS' [Journeyman Smith] trademark. How can life be bad when you get to make knives every day?"

Jody Muller's medieval hand engraving almost covers up the fact that the "DragonMaster" is an automatic knife, complete with sterling-silver "Merlin sphere" button for springing the mosaic-damascus blade into action.

Even the button that fires the ATS-34 blade on Andy Shinosky's double-action automatic folder is highly engraved. The black-lip-pearl handle pools up within its 24k-gold-engraved surroundings.

That Andy Shinosky has been a part-time knifemaker since 1991 is easier to believe than the fact of him being a part-time engraver since 1996. For most, it takes much longer to acquire the skills of a master engraver. The fully engraved handle, including 24k-gold steel scratching, is an impressive entity, as is the leaf-shaped ATS-34 blade of Shinosky's locking-liner folder.

Like a lesson in flowing lines, shapes and patterns, Kelly Carlson's "Ellipse" folder struts its stuff using a black-lip-pearl handle, 14k-gold screws, sterling silver bolsters engraved by Tim George and a 2 ¾-inch Mike Norris stainless damascus blade working off a locking-liner action.

Not bad for a beginner—RUSS SUTTON attended a GRS basic engraving class taught by master engraver Rick Eaton in September 2005. "The class was an exceptional experience that I would highly recommend to anyone interested in learning to engrave," Sutton says.

"Although knife engraving continues to be a learning experience requiring practice, practice, practice, designing and drawing a scroll pattern that looks 'right' on a particular knife involves a lot of erasing and redrawing," Sutton adds.

Only the third knife that Russ Sutton has engraved, he masterfully scrolled up the bolsters of his locking-liner folder, adding an ATS-34 blade, a mammoth-ivory handle, titanium liners and a ruby-inlaid 14k-gold thumb stud.

Knifemaker Vladimir Pulis commissioned Andrea Pulisova to engrave a Mayan motif in deep relief, adding 24k-gold inlay on the bolsters of a mosaic-damascus fixed blade. Pulis married the artwork with a mammoth-tusk handle. The sheath materials include carved bull bone, snakeskin and sapphires.

(Ivan Cillik photos)

VLADIMIR PULIS lives and works in the town of Kremnica in the Slovak Republic, a place rich in history and blacksmithing tradition. After 15 years of teaching in the blacksmithing department of the local university, Pulis decided to devote his time exclusively to knifemaking and decorative metalwork.

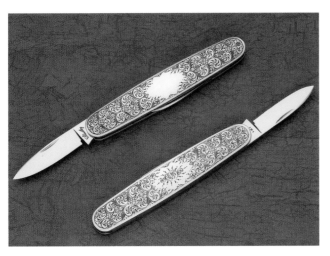

EUGENE SHADLEY planned the perfect art project for a knifemaker with his innate skills and ability—he would make five traditional, all-steel, senator-pattern, two-blade pocketknives. One knife would be given to each of five (four are shown) engravers who'd be asked to do their best work, free of any limitations or budgets, on the gentleman's style pocketknives.

"The idea was for each of the artists to use his or her imagination and skills on an identical form with the hope that the distinctive approaches would be interesting to see and to celebrate," Shadley explains.

The resulting contributions by Simon Lytton, Tim George, Julie Warenski, Amayak Stepanyan and Gil Rudolph undeniably speak to the high quality of the engravers' art today. **(Hoffman photos)**

Dusty Moulton's "Nightwing" features a carved-box-elder-burl handle, a CPM 154CM blade and a 416 stainless steel finger guard that he engraved himself. (KnifeArt.com photo)

Despite the drop-dead-gorgeous fossil-mammoth-tooth handle, Dusty Moulton hopes people will still notice the 416 stainless steel finger guard he engraved. Dusty uses Crucible's new CPM 164CM stainless steel. (**Moulton photo**)

DUSTY MOULTON took a slightly different approach from most novices in learning the knifemaking craft and the art of engraving. "I didn't realize that other knifemakers took apprenticeships to learn the cutlery and engraving crafts," he says. "I gathered as much reading material as I could get my hands on and dove headfirst into knifemaking as a full-time job. I guess I did it right, as 18 months later, at the Oregon Custom Knife Show, I won 'Best New Maker,' 'Best Art Knife' and 'Best in Show' awards.

"I later expanded my self-teaching and dove headlong again into teaching myself engraving, and more recently, the skill of sculpting handles. I feel that each step I add helps to further enhance the value and beauty of the knives. And the fact that the knives are products of my sole authorship will, in the future, give them higher resale value," he continues.

"I have, over the years, developed a style all my own, and I am continually striving to recreate new and old models into a specific, almost organic shape that flows from tip to hilt," Moulton adds.

Dusty Moulton did more than make the knife—he file worked the Jim Ferguson damascus blade, engraved the stainless bolsters and grooved the mammoth-ivory grip. **(SharpByCoop.com photo)**

Gripping the carved-elephant-ivory handle is a pleasure for which Dusty Moulton hopes some interested investor will take advantage. Dusty helps his cause by engraving the finger guard and adding mosaic handle pins. **(Moulton photo)**

THE MOST DASHING OF DAGGERS

With 20 years of blade forging under his belt, WALLY HAYES has developed his own knifemaking style, and creates patterns ranging from tactical fixed blades and folders to high-end damascus daggers and swords. "I have a true love of Japanese-style blades and always go back to working on that style," he says.

OPPOSITE: *Jean-Jose Tritz forged a San-Mai damascus dagger blade, forge welding a tool-steel core and nickel-and-tool-steel outer layers. The guard is 1,500-layer damascus, complemented by an African-blackwood handle and a sterling silver sheath. The fuller (groove along the length of the damascus blade) was cut by hand. Tritz used no machines or epoxy, but rather pinned the handle halves together for a tight fit.*
(Lutz Hoffmeister photos)

American Bladesmith Society master smith Wally Hayes forged a 300-layer damascus blade, 10 inches in length, for his Japanese-style dagger. The piece also showcases copper fittings, including a copper dragon menuki (handle charm), and a silk-wrapped, stingray-skin handle.
(PointSeven photo)

Several artists collaborated on Australian knifemaker David Brodziak's dagger, including Shawn McIntyre, who forged the mosaic-damascus blade before Brodziak ground, shaped, honed and finished it. Richard Chapman engraved the bronze guard, and jeweler Todd Moore fused gold and silver onto antiqued silver in a contemporary art design for the fittings of the dagger and sheath. The smoky-quartz stone inlays are hand cut and faceted, and the handle and sheath are fashioned from the Australian timber "york gum burl."

In 1989, DAVID BRODZIAK started making knives from his home in Albany on the south coast of Western Australia. He is a member of the Australian Knifemakers Guild and has earned an excellent reputation for his fine craftsmanship among knife collectors and enthusiasts, both nationally and internationally.

David works with world-renowned artist Carol Ann O'Connor and knife engraver Richard Chapman, a unique combination that has produced a spectacular range of art knives. Custom orders are welcome and take approximately four to six weeks to complete.

The only two existing knives that Ron Lake and Dietmar Kressler collaborated on, the dashing integral daggers don premium stag grips and oval handle shields.
(Francesco Pachi photo)

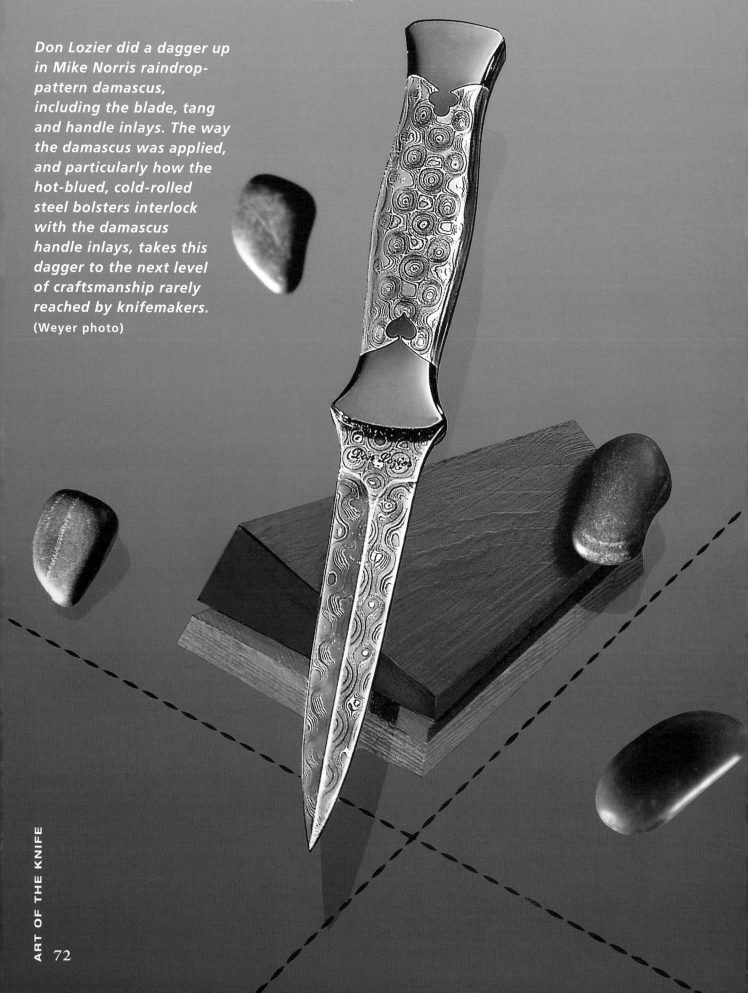

Don Lozier did a dagger up in Mike Norris raindrop-pattern damascus, including the blade, tang and handle inlays. The way the damascus was applied, and particularly how the hot-blued, cold-rolled steel bolsters interlock with the damascus handle inlays, takes this dagger to the next level of craftsmanship rarely reached by knifemakers. (Weyer photo)

You could call it "Tschager's Dagger," and it would certainly be appropriate. The stunning piece is by Reinhard Tschager who incorporated a Johannes Ebner damascus blade, a checkered-ebony handle with mosaic pins, and a stainless steel guard inlaid with mother-of-pearl and embellished with a carved sterling silver mask.

The true character of the dagger lies within the grains and lines of the mammoth-ivory handle and damascus blade. (Ward photo)

RUSTY POLK'S list prices for his knives range from $200 to $1,500 each and he specializes in building bowies, fighters, daggers and hunting knives. He enjoys forging blades, particularly damascus, makes his own sheaths and is beginning to fashion folding knives.

A butcher for the past 14 years, Polk says, "It is one job in which you get to work with your hands and play with knives. I love knives and the art that goes with making them. Being a knifemaker is one of the best jobs, if for no other reason than the friends and customers you meet, as well as the opportunity it presents to work with your hands and create art."

The "Lace Leg Dagger" by Anders Hogstrom parades a 9 ¼-inch, clay-tempered 1050 blade, a black-ebony handle, and textured and antiqued copper fittings. The sheath is lace casuarinas burl treated with a high-gloss finish.

The first knife in Anders Hogstrom's Navy series, this piece is inspired by the shape of a maritime carvel nail tool. The blade is clay-tempered 1050 steel married with a mammoth-bone handle, a damascus spacer and textured-copper fittings.
(BladeGallery.com photo)

ANDERS HOGSTROM
tends to make mostly daggers, fighters and short, guard-less belt knives that he calls "kwaikens." "I make swords and folders, as well, but with less frequency," he notes. "Exotic hardwoods and ancient ivories from all over the world suffice for handles and sheaths. A couple of favorites are Masur birch, for its many different grain patterns and colors, and redwood burl for its sometimes silky appearance.

"I have more wood and fossil ivory in stock than I know what to do with, but I'm always hunting for new, unusual pieces to add to my collection," Hogstrom adds. "I always want to have the right piece on hand when a project comes along."

Scott Slobodian's "Wish" is a ken dagger made using 1050 high-carbon steel, a leather-wrapped handle, Merlin gold fittings and a bubinga-wood saya (sheath). Check out the wavy hamon (temper line) on each side of the center blade ridge.

(Slobodian photo)

BILL AND NANCY HERNDON built a series of four "Rose Daggers" that qualify as true one-of-a-kind masterpieces, not only for their beauty and utility, but also because of the difficulty factor in creating the works of art. The daggers parade rose-bud-shaped pommels, rose-leaf-looking guards, painted porcelain handles and silver or porcelain sheaths.

The porcelain had to be cast in plaster molds, and Nancy's curing, glazing and painting required multiple firings. Each firing caused the porcelain to move, shrink, twist and bend. It required that Bill make 21 sheaths so that he'd end up with four good ones, and 20 handles to achieve four adequate grips.

The guards and pommels were carved from wax and rubber molds. That way Bill could cast wax duplicates of the carvings that were then cast in silver. Nancy, who has been painting porcelain longer than Bill has been making knives, painted the handles and sheaths.

The four resulting daggers (one is not shown) were made for a collector near Tacoma, Wash., but are no longer in his possession. If anyone knows where the knives are, Bill would love to hear from you! His contact information is included in the "Contacts" section at the back of this book.

Shown are three of Bill and Nancy Herndon's "Rose Daggers" featuring rose-bud-shaped pommels, rose-leaf-looking guards, painted porcelain handles and silver or porcelain sheaths. The damascus blades are forged from 5160 and L-6 steels and folded to 320 layers. The stainless steel blade (opposite page) is 440C, and all the blades stretch 4 ¾ inches in length.

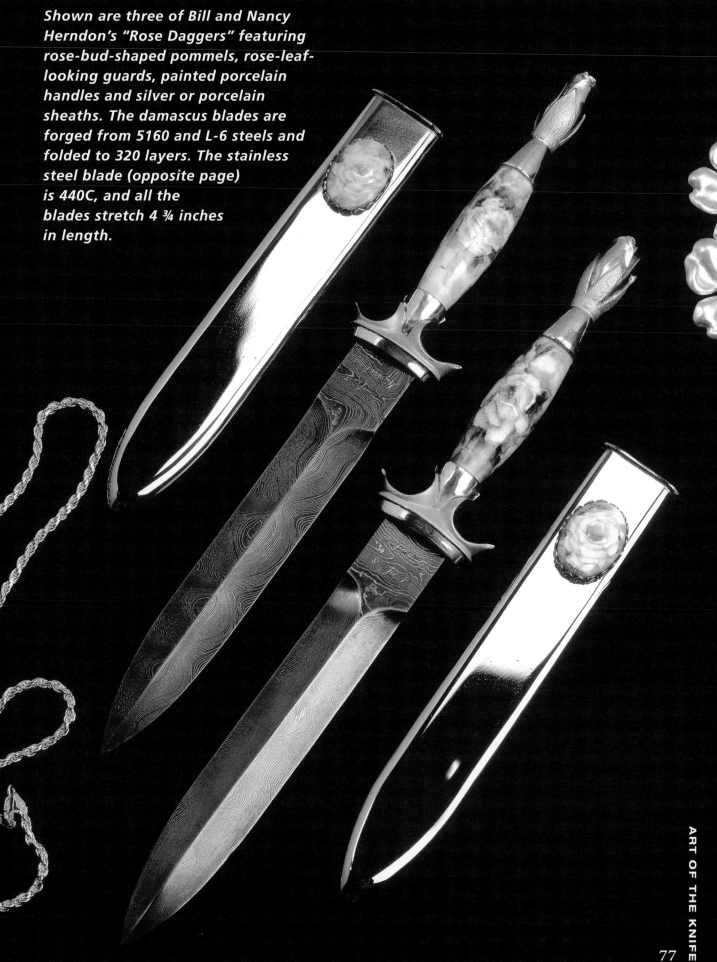

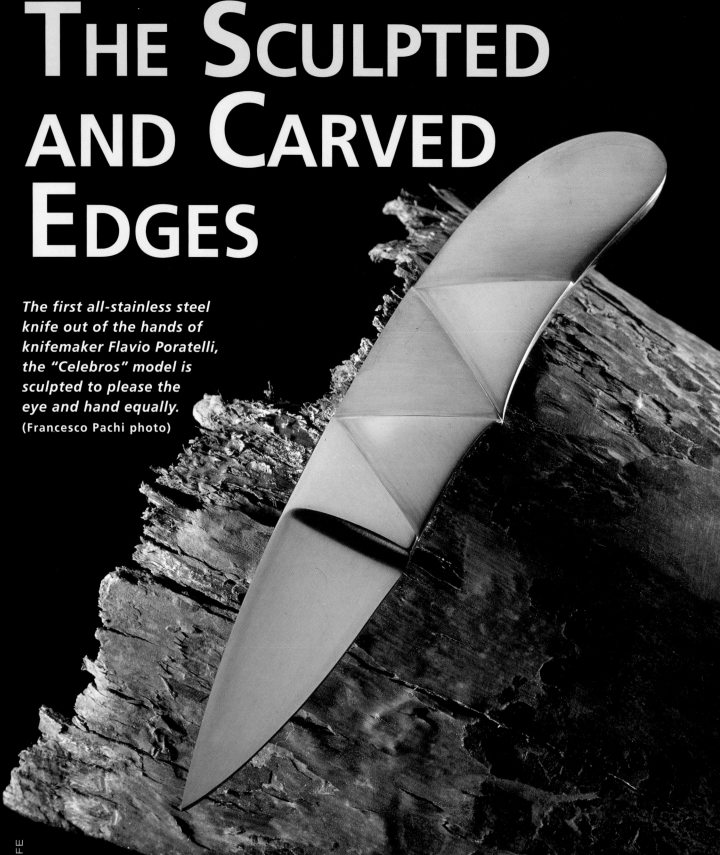

THE SCULPTED AND CARVED EDGES

The first all-stainless steel knife out of the hands of knifemaker Flavio Poratelli, the "Celebros" model is sculpted to please the eye and hand equally.
(Francesco Pachi photo)

Right: The colors of the stabilized box-elder-burl handle are brought out through Garth Hindmarch's stylish use of copper bolsters, mosaic pins and plain, highly polished stainless steel.

Art and utility meet in "Hercules and the Nemean Lion," a fully carved, integral knife from the hands of Arpad Bojtos. And what hands they are! Arpad carved the 440C blade in the likeness of Hercules astride a lunging lion. The handle is fossil walrus ivory complemented by a diamond-inlaid gold band. Hercules and the lion star again, in perfect 3-D form, on the moose-antler, buffalo-horn, gold and silver sheath. **(PointSeven photo)**

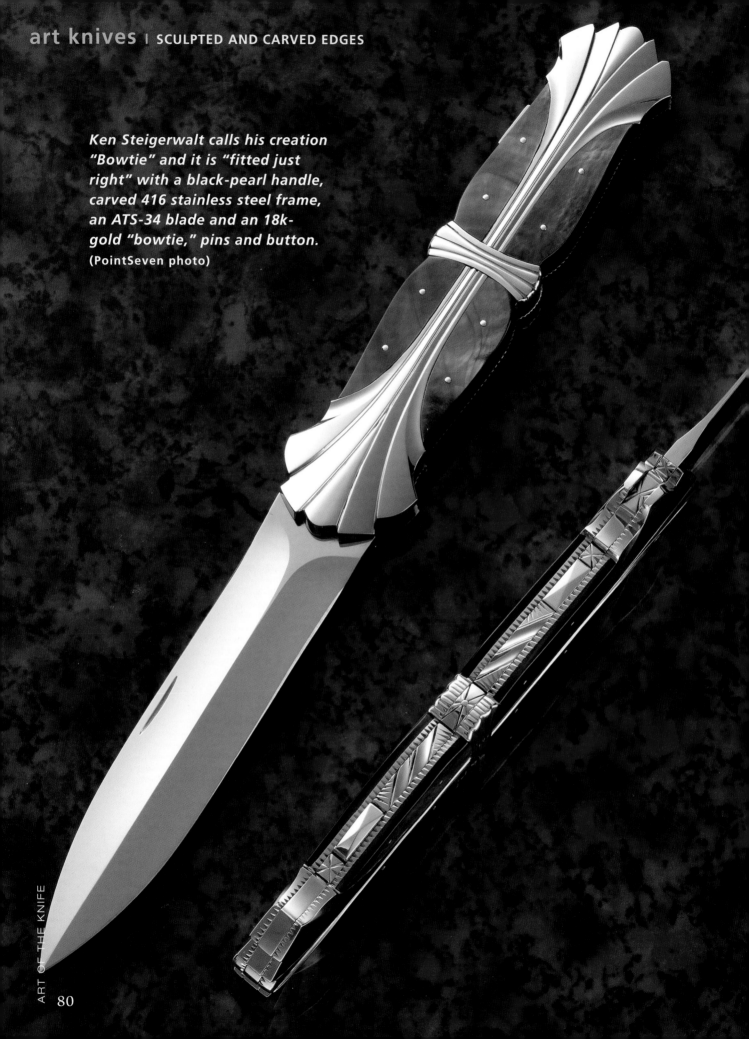

Ken Steigerwalt calls his creation
"Bowtie" and it is "fitted just
right" with a black-pearl handle,
carved 416 stainless steel frame,
an ATS-34 blade and an 18k-
gold "bowtie," pins and button.
(PointSeven photo)

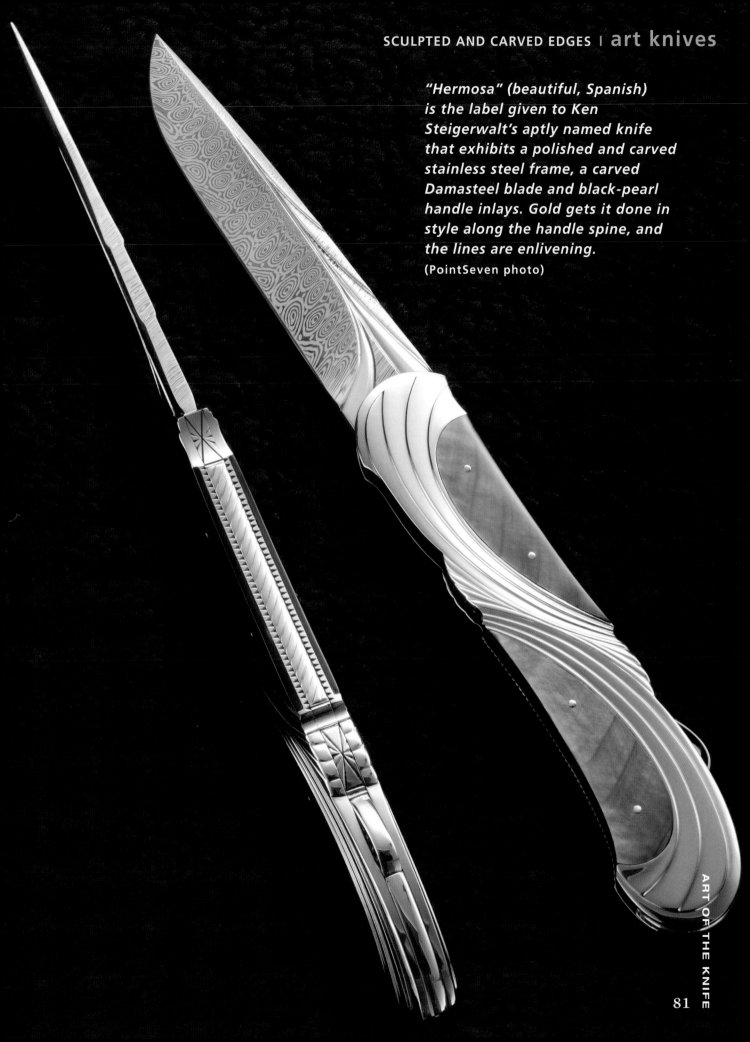

"Hermosa" (beautiful, Spanish) is the label given to Ken Steigerwalt's aptly named knife that exhibits a polished and carved stainless steel frame, a carved Damasteel blade and black-pearl handle inlays. Gold gets it done in style along the handle spine, and the lines are enlivening. (PointSeven photo)

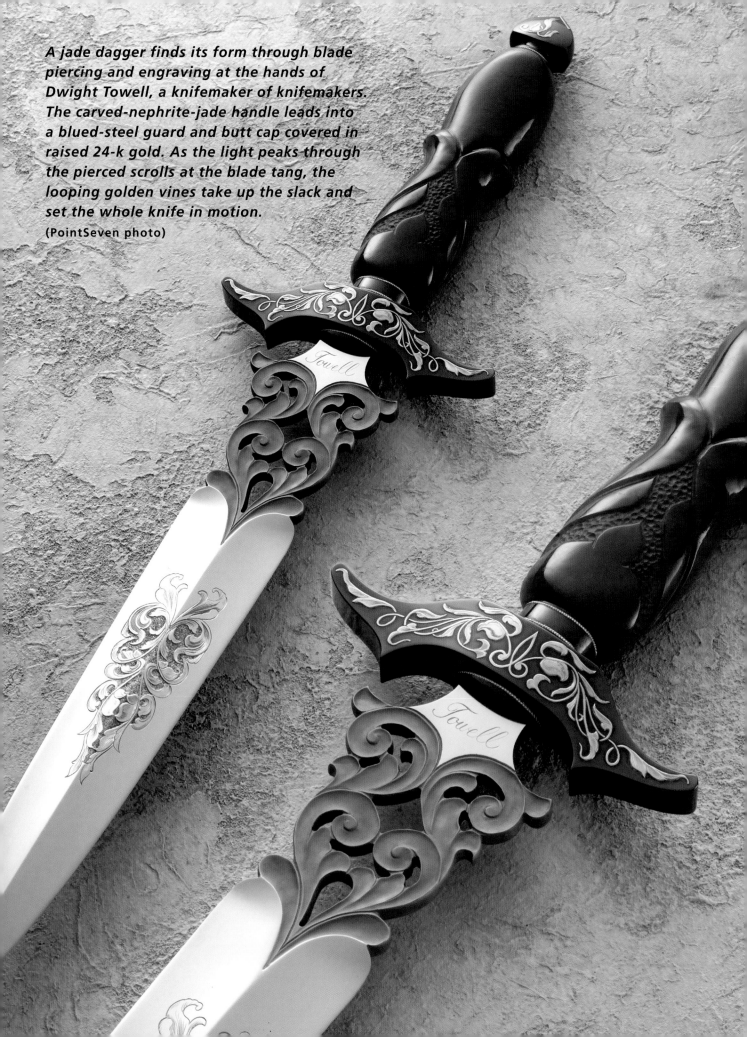

A jade dagger finds its form through blade piercing and engraving at the hands of Dwight Towell, a knifemaker of knifemakers. The carved-nephrite-jade handle leads into a blued-steel guard and butt cap covered in raised 24-k gold. As the light peaks through the pierced scrolls at the blade tang, the looping golden vines take up the slack and set the whole knife in motion.

(PointSeven photo)

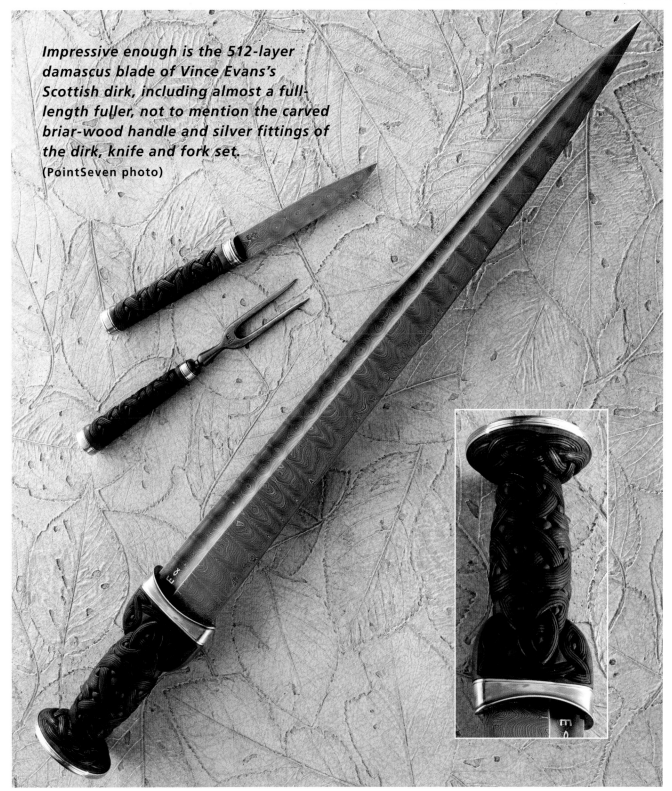

Impressive enough is the 512-layer damascus blade of Vince Evans's Scottish dirk, including almost a full-length fuller, not to mention the carved briar-wood handle and silver fittings of the dirk, knife and fork set.
(PointSeven photo)

Schools and classes that teach Old World embellishment techniques, particularly in regards to sword making, do not exist, according to sword maker VINCE EVANS, so he has learned much of what he knows through experimentation and examining original pieces in museums and private collections.

"Handling original swords and seeing the craftsmanship that went into each piece inspire me to keep learning and experimenting, to understand the craftsman and, in some ways, to touch the past," he says.

With a 30-year background in metal-smithing, jewelry model making and sculpting, STEPHEN OLSZEWSKI has been building knives for eight years now, but by looking at his works of art, you'd think he'd been at it for half a century. "The embellishing and design just seem to come easy for me," he says, "as a result of my background. I really enjoy figure carving and sculpting. Ever since I was a young boy, I have been intrigued by good sculpting. The idea that an artist could create a piece of art, or likeness, in 3-D always amazed me.

"I started at an early age whittling and carving wood," he continues. "Of course, I used a pocketknife to do this with, as do most beginners. Ironic that I would have used a folding knife to carve figures at a young age, only to carve figures into folding knives as an adult!

"I really like nature and animas as subjects. Also, the human form is a good challenge to reproduce," Olszewski notes. "I feel that a sculptor's greatest challenge is to reproduce a beautiful

Stephen Oszewski worked his magic on the Jerry Rados Turkish-twist-damascus bolsters, deep-relief-carving them into oak-leaf and acorn patterns, with deep-etched backgrounds. The blade is Rados damascus, as well, complemented by black-lip-pearl handle scales, a gold bail and file-worked titanium liners. (PointSeven photo)

woman. To carve a female form isn't as difficult as it is to make her pretty. I am also influenced by the early Renaissance masters. How wonderful was their work. A lot of their work is great subject mater for a knife or knife handle.

"As I browse books and art galleries, I am always looking at the art work through 'knife-colored glasses,'" Olszewski jests. "I do a lot of 'figural'-style knives, as well as fully deep-relief-carved pieces. Many of my knives are mistaken as deeply engraved, but they are really deep relief carved.

"I use a lot of rotary tools with carbide burs to rough out the work. Then I switch to files and stones to smoothen out the work. Then a lot of elbow grease with sandpaper comes next. Finally, it's off to the buffing wheel. This is a labor-intensive process," Olszewski explains, "but the finished product is worth the extra work."

"Beguiled" is Stephen Olszewski's latch-release, automatic, locking-liner folder with Jerry Rados Turkish-twist-damascus bolsters deep-relief-carved to depict Eve being tempted by the serpent to eat the forbidden fruit. The blade is Robert Eggerling flame-pattern damascus, and the handle is black-lip pearl. (PointSeven photo)

Named "Floral Enchantment" because of the many floral patterns present throughout the knife, Donald Vogt's locking-liner folder is exceptionally engraved and carved. The hand-carved black-lip-pearl handle scales are sandwiched between carved-14k-gold overlays of leaves. Vogt even carved the Mike Norris "gator-skin-damascus" blade, butting it up against Fox Valley Forge "alien-landscape-pattern" damascus bolsters. A 14k-gold, engraved ring hangs off the back of the knife, in close proximity to the spine of the knife where rubies are inset in engraved gold. Inside the knife handle is a carved 14k-gold scroll engraved with the maker's name. **(PointSeven photo)**

"I started my first knife in 1991 and completed only six pieces by 1995," DONALD VOGT admits. "I was working full time and going to school at night, leaving little time for knifemaking. Each knife was very different in style and process. It gave me a wide view of knifemaking and provided the basics and the desire to expand on my designs."

The "Rattler" automatic knife is a Donald Vogt single-action auto with a Devin Thomas damascus blade and Robert Eggerling damascus bolsters, all carved, of course, by the knifemaker using chisels and a chase hammer. "On the outside of the spine [the top of the knife], there are eight 14k-gold inlays with rubies in them, engraving, and brown-lip-pearl inlays inside and outside the knife," Vogt notes. "The knife has 21 rubies set in 14k gold." **(PointSeven photo)**

Donald Vogt specializes in fashioning folding knives, using only the best materials in his designs. He embellishes knives with gold, jewels, pearl inlays and abalone. He fully carves each piece from front to back using graver chisels and a chase hammer. "When I create a knife, I make a drawing of it, sizing it the way I want it, and include how the knife will be carved in the sketch," Vogt explains.

The carved hawk-bill-style Mike Norris gator-skin-damascus blade is impressive enough, but check out the carved, multi-colored Robert Eggerling damascus bolsters of Donald Vogt's folding knife. The bolsters are heat colored blue, purple and copper, and are the centerpiece of the knife, sandwiched between the blade and a carved gold-lip-pearl handle. Other features include two engraved 14k-gold inlays inset with rubies, abalone inlays along the knife spine, a 14k-gold ring and color-anodized liners. (PointSeven photo)

"I carve each piece of a knife separately from the other pieces by screwing a part to a metal plate held in a PanaVise so the piece can be turned and/or tilted. Cleanup is done with needle files, sandpaper and a great deal of patience," Donald Vogt says. "Everything is made to mate up, and both sides of the knife match."

Gold pins on the handle and blade of Robert Weinstock's art folder are just an added touch to the carved and sculpted damascus showpiece. (Francesco Pachi photo)

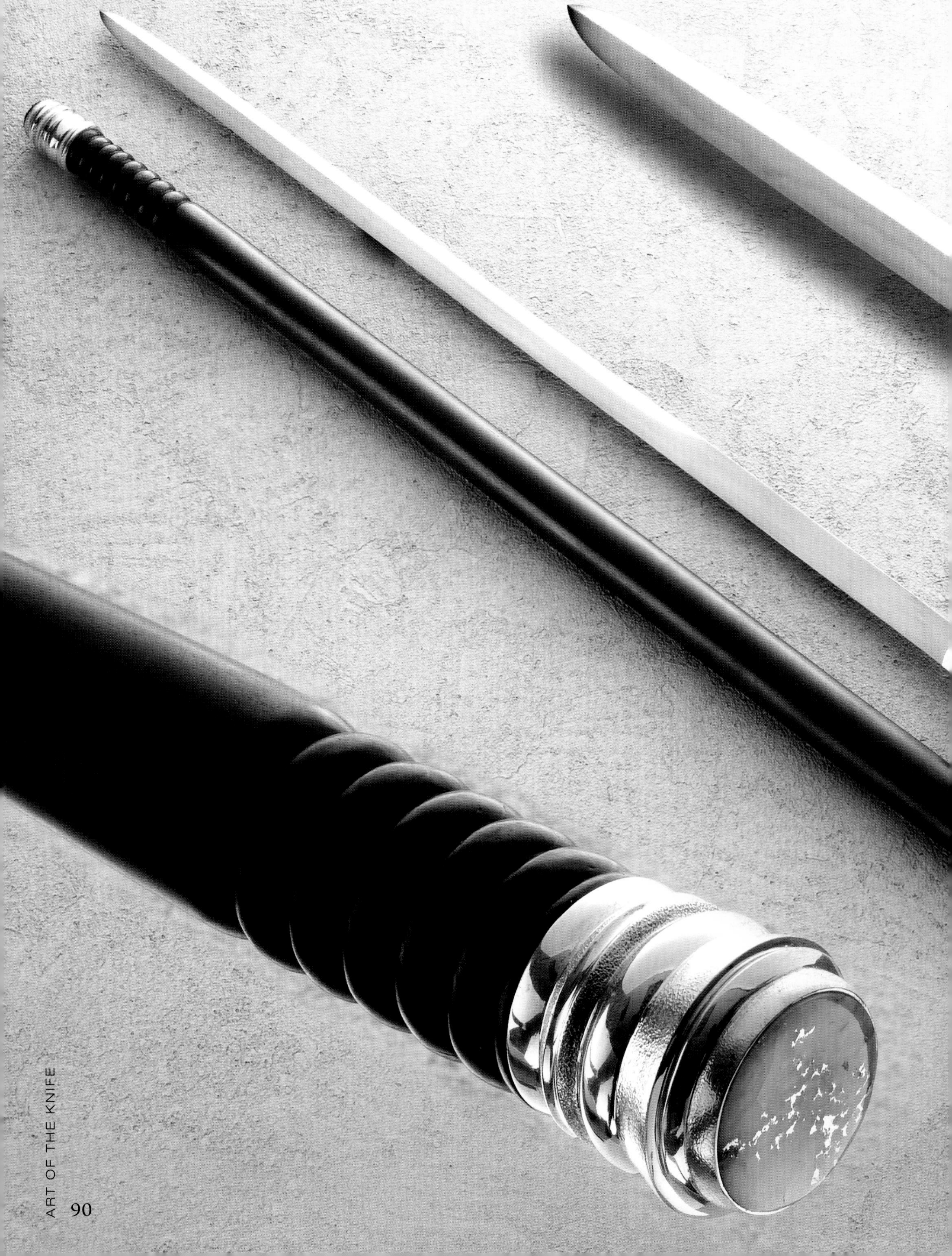

*Both of David Goldberg's
Shikomi-Zue sword canes,
on pages 90-93, feature
hand-carved ebony sayas
(sheaths). The piece on this
page boasts a solid-silver
habaki (blade collar), and a
fuchi (handle fitting) of solid
sterling silver and 18k-gold
set with pure gold quartz.*
(PointSeven photos)

David Goldberg's "Shogun" is a double-edged Ken-style piece showcasing a two-piece habaki of solid 18k rose and green gold. The rose gold section features red plique-a-jour enamel set with a ruby and diamonds on both sides. The green section is cloisonné enamel in yellow and blue. The guard is solid sterling silver in a chrysanthemum motif; the 18k-gold menuki (hilt ornaments) are of a double-claw motif; and the tsuka (handle) is Gaboon ebony wood covered with stingray skin and wrapped in polished leather cord. **(PointSeven photos)**

David Goldberg's "Full Moon Raven" exhibits a carved solid-sterling-silver tsuba (guard) in a "four lobe" motif, carved sterling silver menuki (hilt ornaments) in a raven motif and more carved sterling fuchi/kashira (handle fittings) in cherry-tree-and-moon and clouds motifs. The case is lacquered magnolia wood that encloses the differentially hardened, single-edge Hira Zukuri style blade. **(PointSeven photo)**

Imagine carving the basket motif into the solid-sterling-silver handle of the Kozuka (utility knife). David Goldberg did just that, complementing it with an 18k-gold hilt ornament and a velvet-lined Honduran rosewood case featuring an 18k-gold "gold mountain forge logo." **(PointSeven photo)**

A one-of-a-kind automatic knife, both the 3 ½-inch, heat-colored Robert Eggerling damascus blade and the heat-colored O-1 snake "tongue" are powered via a coil spring and activated by a push button. **(PointSeven photo)**

PHILIP BOOTH says the coolest thing about his "Serpentine Rattler" is what you can't see—a space under the carved, textured and colored ancient-ivory handle that he hollowed out and filled with many tiny ball bearings so that when you shake the knife it rattles like the snake that it is.

SHIVA

Shiva Ki is a bladesmith unafraid to express his creative side by building, in his words, "the primo battle blade." It includes a carved-impala-horn handle and a 9 ½-inch blade.
(PointSeven photo)

Any crocodile hunter would be privileged to grip the carved-cocobolo handle of Shiva Ki's wild fixed blade involving 10 inches of tempered and etched blade steel. (PointSeven photo)

The singular eel-like, carved snakewood handle of Paolo Scordia's Murena model is highly figured and finely finished. (Francesco Pachi photo)

The collaborative work of RALF HOFFMANN and SABINE PIPER is strongly influenced by the Japanese art philosophy "less is more." Hoffmann was a goldsmith, making jewelry for nearly 30 years. Since 1989, he has experimented with Japanese metal techniques and carving netsuke.

In 1985, he learned to forge damascus and started to make knives.

Piper is a designer who worked for more than 15 years for advertising agencies. In 1996 she took up sculpture, working in stone, wood and bronze. Hoffman began teaching her to forge damascus in 2001. Since then, both have worked together. They work from their own knife sketches and models, building each one-of-a-kind knife by hand, forging the damascus and performing all the steps and processes themselves.

The handles are carved from wood, metal, damascus, stone, ivory and mokumé gane.

Most of the output is in the form of fighters and swords, or small folding knives with animal-shaped handles inspired by Japanese netsuke.

Ralf Hoffmann and Sabine Piper forged the integral damascus "Velolurch" art knife, hand carving the piece and giving it the form of a lizard. Two types of damascus steel— a 2,000-layer pattern for the blade, and a lizard-skin-looking "Spiro-pattern" damascus for the handle and tail—are forged welded together. The eyes are citrine stones, with the pupils carved and colored black. The knife blade slides into a "bike saddle" wooden stand when not in use.

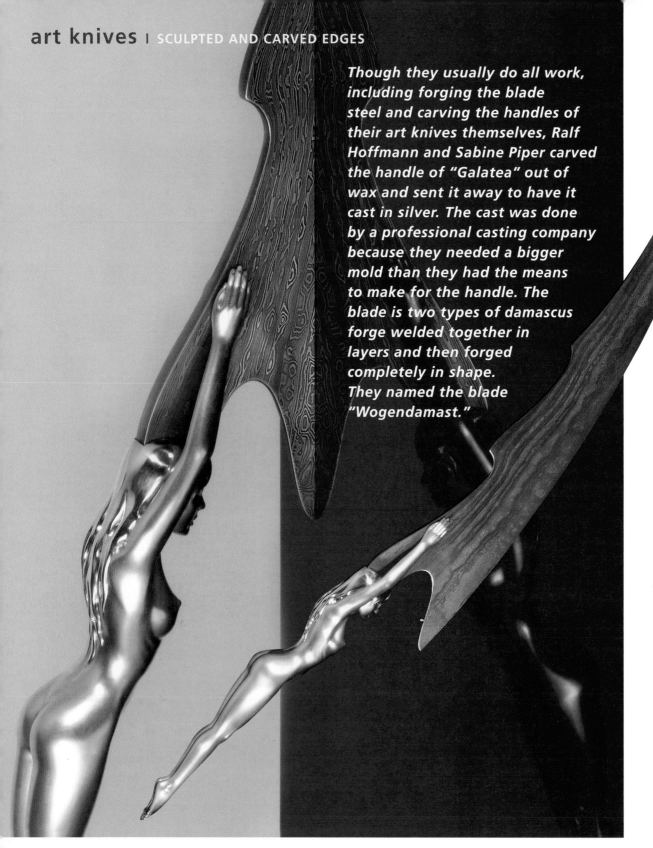

Though they usually do all work, including forging the blade steel and carving the handles of their art knives themselves, Ralf Hoffmann and Sabine Piper carved the handle of "Galatea" out of wax and sent it away to have it cast in silver. The cast was done by a professional casting company because they needed a bigger mold than they had the means to make for the handle. The blade is two types of damascus forge welded together in layers and then forged completely in shape. They named the blade "Wogendamast."

Galatea is a figure known in Greek mythology, one of the "nereiden"—the daughters of Poseidon—and she is the most beautiful of all. It is a creature who can live in water as on earth, and nobody understands exactly how it lived. There is much speculation, but the imagination is the only limit. Thus, HOFFMANN and PIPER created a photo showing Galatea diving from one world into another. It is the wish of all of us, they speculate, to be in a better world or a better time.

Lovers, one of human form and one winged, hide their faces, but not in shame, never in shame when so naturally beautiful. Sculpting or carving steel into such fantastic forms, using only hand files, skill and ingenuity is an art not lost on the masters, and particularly not on knifemaker Arpad Bojtos. The knife is inlaid with gold, copper and titanium; the handle fashioned from fossil walrus ivory; and the classically carved sheath, where the lovers reveal their full figures, is ivory, gold and silver. **(PointSeven photo)**

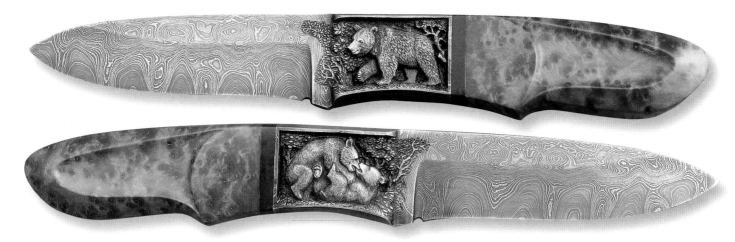

In 1970, Julius Mojzis finished Art and Craft School as a blacksmith where he was trained in engraving and sculpting, two skills that are at the basis of his knifemaking. He built replicas of historic swords before dabbling in damascus blade steel. He forges damascus blades from chains and chain saw blades, as well as carving and engraving knives for other makers. He specializes in carving animals in miniature, as is the case with the bears at play on the integral damascus blade of the burl-handle masterpiece.

"My knives are hand forged of high-carbon tool steel. After each blade is ground to shape, it is hardened and differentially tempered, the latter process giving it a hard edge with a slightly softer spine for a tough yet flexible blade that won't chip or break," explains KARL SCHROEN. "A low-melt silver solder is used when attaching a knife guard so nothing can penetrate or damage the handle material. I use dense exotic woods, and various types of horn and ivory as knife handles. These are pinned and glued to the blade tang."

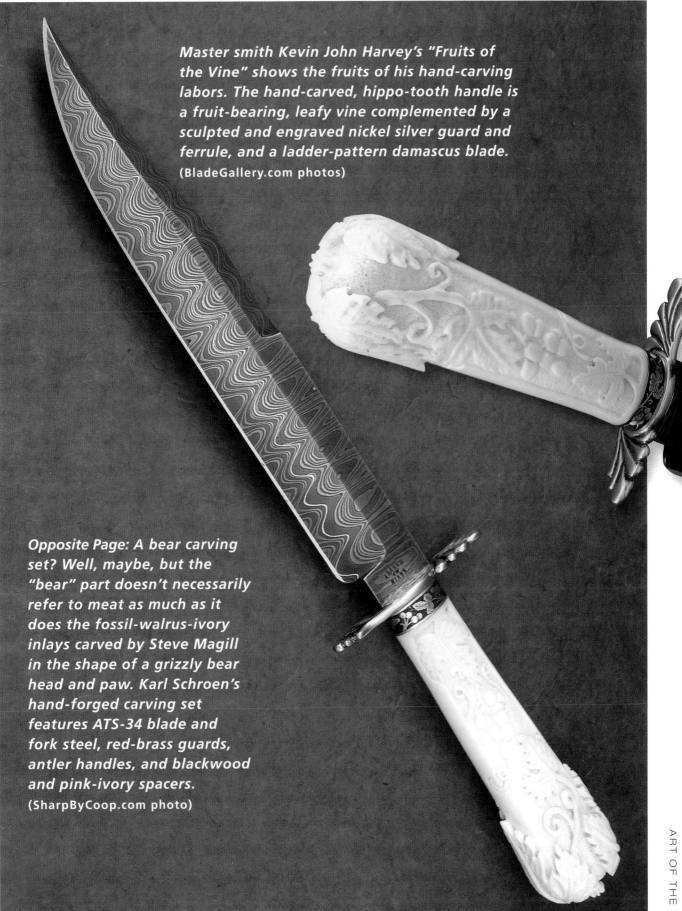

Master smith Kevin John Harvey's "Fruits of the Vine" shows the fruits of his hand-carving labors. The hand-carved, hippo-tooth handle is a fruit-bearing, leafy vine complemented by a sculpted and engraved nickel silver guard and ferrule, and a ladder-pattern damascus blade. (BladeGallery.com photos)

Opposite Page: A bear carving set? Well, maybe, but the "bear" part doesn't necessarily refer to meat as much as it does the fossil-walrus-ivory inlays carved by Steve Magill in the shape of a grizzly bear head and paw. Karl Schroen's hand-forged carving set features ATS-34 blade and fork steel, red-brass guards, antler handles, and blackwood and pink-ivory spacers. (SharpByCoop.com photo)

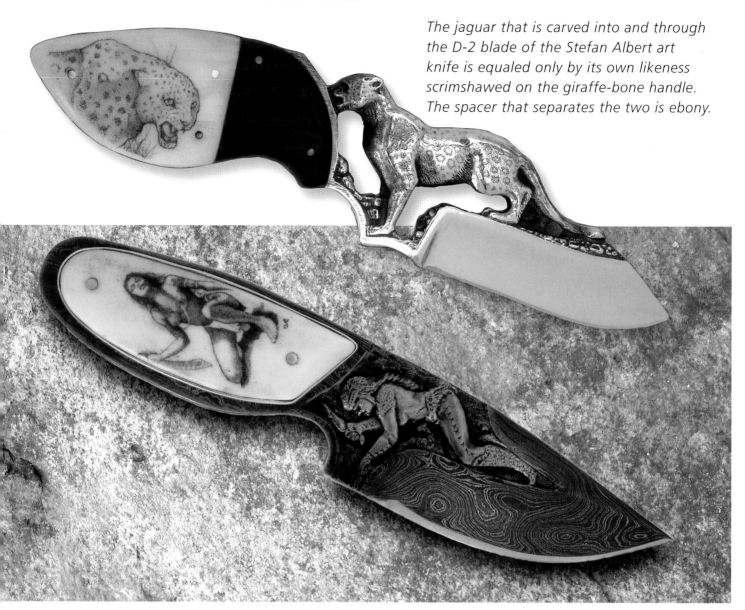

The jaguar that is carved into and through the D-2 blade of the Stefan Albert art knife is equaled only by its own likeness scrimshawed on the giraffe-bone handle. The spacer that separates the two is ebony.

Though Vladimir Pulis is credited for forging the damascus blade, it is friend and confidant Stefan Albert who carved the blade-bearing femme into the steel, and gave her life via scrimshaw on an antler handle overlay.

VIRGIL ENGLAND'S blades (bottom of opposite page) are forged from iron sands or billets, made by DARYL MEIER to England's specifications, which Virgil then forges to shape. "Daryl Meier and I have been working together for 17 years, with him hand forge-welding the 'heart' of each piece," England notes. "It is important that each blade be truly functional, and therefore structural integrity is of prime importance.

"The patterning in my blades is usually the result of manipulation through forging of random billets where the individual layers are initially parallel to each other," England continues. "This induces 'ghost' or 'phantom' light refraction, which is caused by individual hammer blows, as seen most often in the Kris blades of Indonesia."

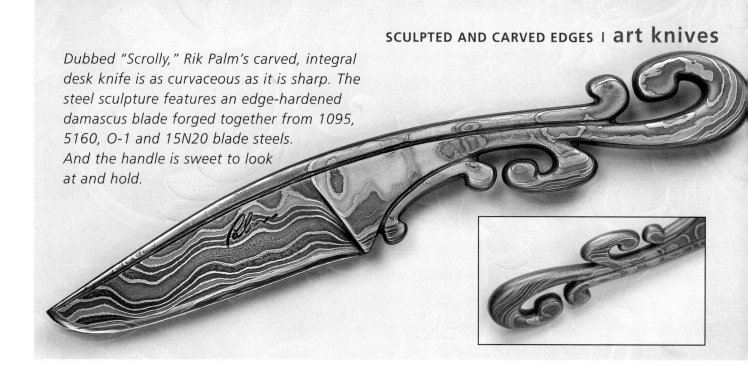

Dubbed "Scrolly," Rik Palm's carved, integral desk knife is as curvaceous as it is sharp. The steel sculpture features an edge-hardened damascus blade forged together from 1095, 5160, O-1 and 15N20 blade steels. And the handle is sweet to look at and hold.

Below: Virgil England forged the damascus blade of the "Kraaken" fighter to shape, complementing it with bronze, mammoth ivory, Madagascar ebony and leather. "I carved and scrimshawed the mammoth-ivory grip to represent overlapping scales," he says. The piece is based on a Pharonic Nile delta form of the early dynasties, the originals of which were used as harvesting tools and weapons.

Opposite Page: Although Gary Root built the knife, unifying the elements and creating a thematic piece, Dr. Paul Grussenmeyer must be credited for his incredible "war eagle" carving of the Sambar stag handle. The 10-inch blade is 300-layer, nine-bar Robert Eggerling compound damascus that has been heat-treated to a patina that complements the redness of the carved-stag grip. The guard is also Eggerling damascus, and Jim Layton fashioned the leather sheath. (SharpByCoop.com photo)

Ron Lake and Wolfgang Loerchner collaborated on two tab-lock folders, each given the serial number "1," and a pair of art knives that has become known in some knife circles. Ron made the knives and mechanisms, and Wolfgang sculpted the handles. (Francesco Pachì photo)

The Wood Handlers

Above: *The silver wire inlay and red-dyed wood work wonders on a curly-maple knife grip. Garth Hindmarch didn't skip such subtle touches as a hammer-textured ricasso and file-worked blade spine.*

GARTH HINDMARCH makes working and fancy straight knives, fillet knives, bowies and friction folders, as well as some presentation knives for various fundraising auctions where he lives. For his own personal edged art collection, he has fashioned 16 reproductions of 19th-century Sheffield and American bowies, his favorite sharp subjects, particularly the Kimball style dog-bone-handled bowie.

Right: *The colors of the stabilized box-elder-burl handle are brought out through Garth Hindmarch's stylish use of copper bolsters, mosaic pins and plain, highly polished stainless steel.*

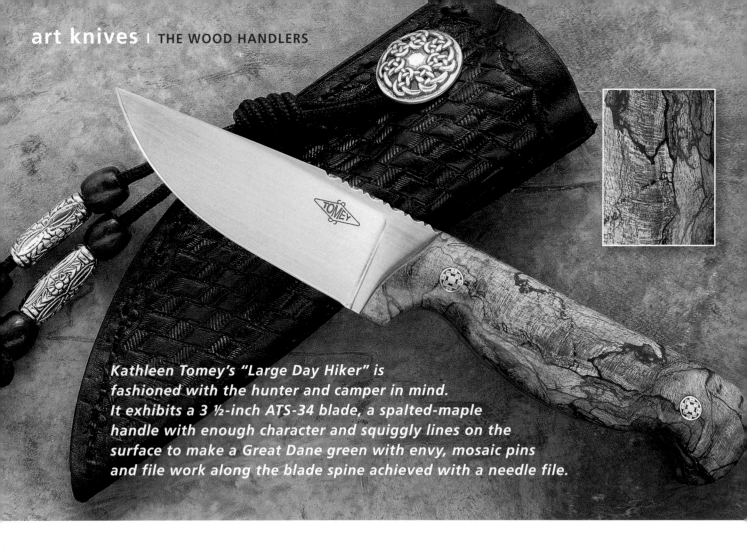

*Kathleen Tomey's "Large Day Hiker" is
fashioned with the hunter and camper in mind.
It exhibits a 3 ½-inch ATS-34 blade, a spalted-maple
handle with enough character and squiggly lines on the
surface to make a Great Dane green with envy, mosaic pins
and file work along the blade spine achieved with a needle file.*

KATHLEEN TOMEY says she grew up in a neighborhood with a lot of boys to
play with, but only one other girl. "We collected knives, whittled sticks, threw knives
at trees and played mumblety-peg with them," she says. "In those days, there was
no age limit on the purchase of knives, and I owned a switchblade at age
13 [my mother didn't know]. I still own a bowie knife that my first
boyfriend gave me about 45 years ago."

*Say howdy to a
dyed and stabilized
black-ash-burl handle that
is everything but black—perhaps
purple, green, orange and blue, but definitely
not black. Kathleen Tomey's sport/utility/camp knife
also features mosaic pins and an ATS-34 blade with
vine-pattern file work along the spine.*

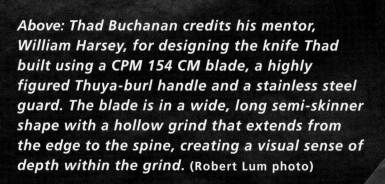

Above: Thad Buchanan credits his mentor, William Harsey, for designing the knife Thad built using a CPM 154 CM blade, a highly figured Thuya-burl handle and a stainless steel guard. The blade is in a wide, long semi-skinner shape with a hollow grind that extends from the edge to the spine, creating a visual sense of depth within the grind. (Robert Lum photo)

The acrylic stabilized-goat-willow handle of Tom Bache-Wiig's integral hunting knife gives it the oomph it needs to take the stainless steel knife to a level of rarely achieved artistry.

Bud Nealy is one of the first makers to realize the necessity of small, concealable knives for use by law enforcement officials and by business executives wishing to protect themselves. He is best known for his patented MCS (Multi-Concealment Sheath) system. Fabricated from Kydex®, it can be outfitted with one of five attachments, offering a variety of carry positions. The red liner of Nealy's "Beladau" fixed blade adds just the right highlight to the pretty purple-heart-wood handle.

The finely finished cocobolo handle of Bud Nealy's "Delaware" model is fastened to the full tang of the ATS-34 blade using hand-fashioned mosaic pins.

BUD NEALY made an abrupt turn into the world of knifemaking 26 years ago, having been a journeyman musician performing in such diverse media as Broadway shows, the ballet, recording studios, and big-band and small-group gigs. After much reading, trial and error, private instruction and university seminars, his knifemaking hobby became a full-time business.

Alberto Symonds harvested the acacia wood for the handle of his damascus skinning knife from his own ranch in Montevideo, Uruguay. The bolsters of the fancy skinner are handmade mokumé.

Alberto Symonds builds a damascus fixed blade that showcases a black-ash handle, nickel silver bolsters and mosaic pins.

"For knife handles, I incorporate a lot of wood from local trees, including fruit trees, all of which grow on my ranch," reports ALBERTO SYMONDS of Uruguay. "In addition, I use olive-tree root from dead trees, which has revealed incredible grains, and I buy exotic woods from suppliers of knife materials."

ART OF THE KNIFE

The red hues of the maple-burl handle are brought out further by the red and gold mosaic pin in the center of the grip, and contrasted by the steel blade and nickel silver guard of Dick Faust's stylish knife.

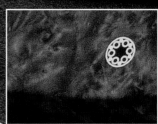

While the box-elder handle of Dick Faust's knife is rounded and bulbous, the 154CM blade is angular, pointed and sharp.

After 20 years as a collector, DICK FAUST became a full-time knifemaker eight years ago. "Inspired by the best, I developed my own style of a handsome but practical working knife," he says. "I do all the work by hand without any help from jigs or fixtures, so my knives are truly handcrafted.

"My hunters and campers are simple in their execution, with hollow-ground blades from 154CM steel, exceptional wood or bone handles, and overall emphasis on fit and finish," Faust adds. "The way a knife feels in the hand is the most important element, allowing it to be used properly and without fatigue."

"I am fortunate to have acquired two early-1900s-era anvils from my maternal and paternal grandfathers, and also a coal forge that is used in the knifemaking process," says C.R. MILES JR. "I have branched out into forging blades using a gas forge built from scratch, so all of my knives are now made from start to finish, including heat treating, in my shop."

C.R. Miles Jr. fashioned an 18th-century-style rifleman's knife from a blackened 1095 high-carbon-steel blade with a tapered tang, a curly maple handle and brass pins. **(Hoffman photo)**

Below: *The blending of a curly maple handle and water-buffalo-horn bolsters makes for a nice transition into the polished stainless steel blade of C.R. Miles Jr.'s skinner.* **(Hoffman photo)**

IRON DOCTOR
Handcrafted Knives
C.R. Miles Jr.
Lugoff, SC

The small fishing knife (top) and skinner feature stabilized-birch-burl handles and powdered-metal, stainless steel blades. Knifemaker Tom Bache-Wiig says the fishing knife fits perfectly in the palm of your hand.

An integral fishing knife, Tom Bache-Wiig's piece was developed using an Uddeholm Elmax powdered-metal blade and an ebony handle. It stretches 8.67 inches overall.

The curly maple handle of
Shiva Ki's re-curved fixed blade
is sanded to a high sheen,
equaling that of the 13-inch
blade. **(PointSeven photo)**

SHIVA

The "tomahawk chop" practiced at Atlanta Braves games would be so much more impressive using Jerry Lairson's hand-fashioned "hawk" that features a curly-maple haft and a damascus head with a wolf-tooth-pattern along the cutting edge.

"I don't do a lot of embellishment on my knives," says JERRY LAIRSON. "I prefer to have them noticed because of their flowing lines, balanced appearance and the use of exotic materials. The beauty can be enhanced by clean work.

"I would rather build a high-performance knife than a beautiful knife but there isn't any reason a knife can't be both," Lairson adds. "When I forge damascus steel for a knife, I pattern it to match the rest of the knife. I want the pattern to complement and blend with the rest of the materials and flow with the shape of the knife. What I'm looking for is a subtle but elegant appearance."

The stabilized-maple-burl handle of the Jerry Lairson "Sultana" is grooved for a good grip and butts up against a damascus guard and spacer, and an 8 ¾-inch raindrop-pattern-damascus blade with a shark's-tooth pattern along the cutting edge.

Rob Hudson outfitted the trailing-point hunter with a maple-burl handle, attaching it to the full tang using six pins, and dovetailed bolsters. Hudson file worked the entire length of the ATS-34 blade and tang.

Above: Rob Hudson's 13-inch bowie boasts a Thuya-burl handle with buffalo-horn spacers, an ATS-34 blade, 416 stainless steel fittings, and guard and pommel engraving by Bruce Shaw.

Left: The combination of turquoise and curly maple makes for a pretty pairing on a Rob Hudson upswept bird knife that also incorporates a stainless-damascus blade, and a stainless steel guard and pommel.

To complement the drop-dead-gorgeous black-palm handle of his custom bush knife, Don Norris commissioned Francine Larstein to etch an African lion scene on the Mountain Forge damascus blade. The D-guard and pommel are also Mountain Forge damascus.
(**PointSeven** photo)

Before selling his business and retiring in 1987, DON NORRIS had traveled extensively for years as a company executive. "I had begun to collect knives and guns in the 1950s, and as a result of the wider market available to me in my travels, I was able to accumulate a substantial collection," Norris relates.

After Norris retired, he visited knifemakers in various locations throughout the country and commissioned custom pieces to be made for him. "My interest in knifemaking was growing and I was constantly reading and studying everything I could get my hands on to increase my knowledge of the art," he says. "I needed a hobby to occupy my time, so in 1989 I went out to the garage, set up some machinery and made my first knife. I was so intrigued that I immediately made two or three more, and thus Norris Custom Knives was born."

Stunning artistry defines Scott Slobodian's tanto as much as its amboyna-wood handle and sheath, sterling-silver furniture engraved in a turtle motif by Scott's wife, Barbara, and clay-tempered 1050 high-carbon-steel blade with wild hamons (temper lines). (Slobodian photo)

Let's start with the buckeye-burl saya (scabbard) of a *Scott Slobodian* Japanese-style piece and move on to the 1,000-layer *Daryl Meier* blade, the sterling-silver habaki (blade collar) and leather-wrapped stingray-skin handle. (Slobodian photo)

Born and raised in Susquehanna, Pa., E. JAY HENDRICKSON spent many of his days as a youth hunting in the endless mountain region, as well as fishing along the Susquehanna River. "I developed a love of knives and handcrafted bows and arrows," Hendrickson relates.

After spending two years in the Army, in Nuremberg, Germany, Jay attended and graduated from Broome Technical Community College in Binghamton, N.Y., and went to work for IBM. "In 1967, my family and I transferred to Frederick, Md., and it was here, in 1974, that I seriously started making knives."

The curly maple handle and matching sheath of E. Jay Hendrickson's small clip-point bowie are decorated in a Southwest Indian design. Such would include fine silver inlay with diamond-shaped nickel silver escutcheons, all complemented by a nickel silver double guard. The 7 ¾-inch blade is W-2 and 203E damascus forged by the maker. **(PointSeven photo)**

This upscale carving knife-and-fork set by Thomas Haslinger has been designed for ease of use, while keeping the overall appearance elegant. Both pieces are perfectly balanced, and the fork is capable of lifting up to 65 pounds. The BG-42 implements feature stabilized-fiddle-back-maple handles and African-blackwood inlays. For the storage box, Haslinger veneered fiddle-back maple over Santo's mahogany, adding subtle detailing with blackwood. The box is lined with black velvet and hand finished with oil. **(BladeGallery.com photo)**

Thomas Haslinger's double-edged "Elm Fighter" is of the size to serve as a small fighter or boot knife, and the Carpathian elm handle is designed so that it can be maneuvered in the hand without discomfort. Haslinger gave the piece a paua-shell inlay a bead-blasted stainless steel guard and a cowhide sheath overlaid with salmon leather. **(T. Haslinger photo)**

ART OF THE KNIFE

125

The stabilized-cherry-burl handle of J. Neilson's "Crooked" camp knife leads into a full 9 ¾ inches of hand-rubbed 5160 spring steel with a ¼-inch spine. The handle bolts and lanyard liner are stainless steel, and the knife comes with the tooled-leather sheath that is shown.

J. Neilson says his "Baby Bola" makes for a great skinner or utility hunter. The blade is forged from 3/16-inch-thick 1095 stock and has a hand-rubbed finish and file-worked spine. The knife is 9 ¾ inches overall with a 4 ½-inch cutting edge. A desert-ironwood handle and tooled-leather pouch sheath complete the package.

J. Neilson's coffin-handle bowie boasts a clay-hardened 1084 blade, a brass guard with file-worked accents, a cocobolo handle and a stabilized-buffalo-horn throat.

THOMAS GERNER was born and grew up in Norway, a country with a long history and tradition of knives and knifemaking, and one that places an emphasis on the knife as a tool. "Although I spent a lot of my youth in the local blacksmith's forge, and have been making knives since the late 80s, I felt a need to learn more," Gerner notes. "In 1993, I attended some courses at the Bill Moran School of Bladesmithing in Washington, Ark., and a couple years later I was granted my journeyman smith stamp from the American Bladesmithing Society. In 2001, I achieved a master smith rating, becoming the first Australian to do so."

Only the spacer of Thomas Gerner's utility knife is wood, but the red ebony makes such an impression, it stands out more than the equally clean and classy red-deer-antler handle and forged L-6 blade.
(Pete Solvander photo, Brand New Design Ltd.)

Thomas Gerner took it upon himself to reproduce a traditional barrel knife by hand. He utilized "bird's-eye" she oak, brass fittings and a forged L-6 blade to accomplish the complicated task.
(Pete Solvander photo, Brand New Design Ltd.)

ART OF THE KNIFE

127

QUITE FASHIONABLE FOLDERS

"In working with knives, I have come to prefer natural handle materials—ivory, mother-of-pearl, stag and bone, among others. And I admit to a love of beautiful damascus steel for art-knife blades," Don Norris says. The locking-liner folder benefits greatly from a mammoth-ivory handle and a Devin Thomas damascus blade that Norris skillfully file worked. Tiger-eye thumb studs, Chris Marks damascus bolsters and jeweled-titanium liners complete the package. (ScreenSurge photo)

In this case, having good fashion sense means building a Devin Thomas "Vines and Roses" pattern stainless-damascus locking-liner folder, complete with Robert Eggerling damascus bolsters, a mammoth-ivory handle, 6 AL-4V titanium liners and gold-plated Torx™ screws. The knifemaker, Terry Knipschield, filed the back spacer into a "flaming thorn" pattern, just for kicks.

(Matt Knipschield photo)

The double exposure of a Ron Lake knife shows both sides of a folder that showcases a premium-stag handle, a gold bail, tab lock and a blade etched with a "mirror logo," in which the maker's name is readable on one side of the blade and backward, or a mirror of itself, on the other side.
(Francesco Pachi photo)

From the collection of Pierluigi Peroni are two Ron Lake lock-back folders, each denoted by serial number "1," and each in the "inter-frame" design for which Lake has become known. The "Sierra" models sport bighorn-sheep (left) and stag handle inlays. (Francesco Pachi photo)

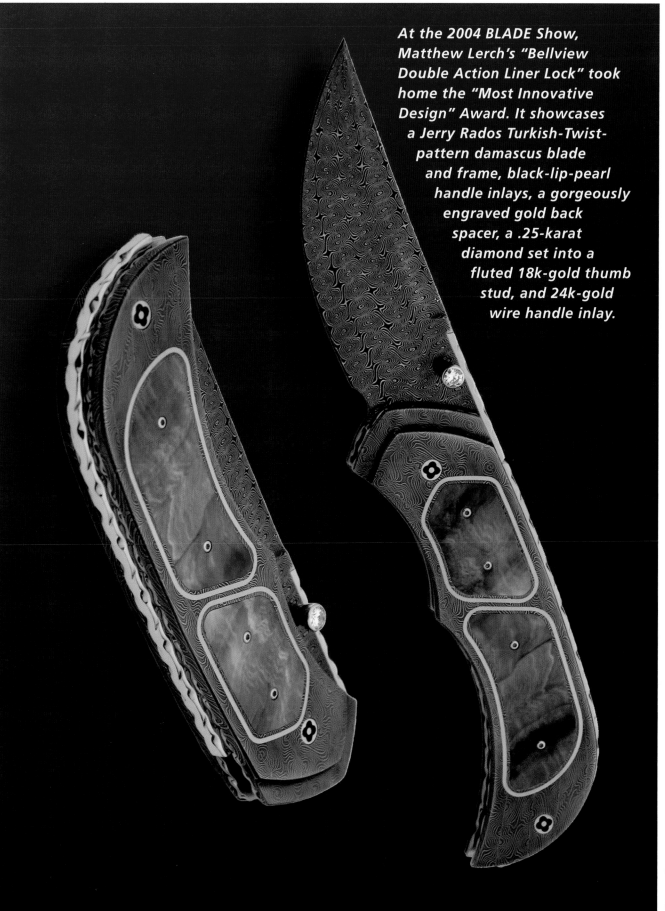

At the 2004 BLADE Show, Matthew Lerch's "Bellview Double Action Liner Lock" took home the "Most Innovative Design" Award. It showcases a Jerry Rados Turkish-Twist-pattern damascus blade and frame, black-lip-pearl handle inlays, a gorgeously engraved gold back spacer, a .25-karat diamond set into a fluted 18k-gold thumb stud, and 24k-gold wire handle inlay.

ART OF THE KNIFE

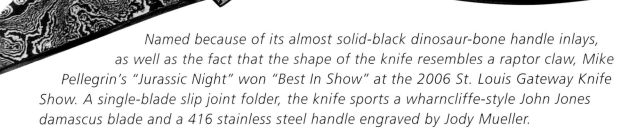

Named because of its almost solid-black dinosaur-bone handle inlays, as well as the fact that the shape of the knife resembles a raptor claw, Mike Pellegrin's "Jurassic Night" won "Best In Show" at the 2006 St. Louis Gateway Knife Show. A single-blade slip joint folder, the knife sports a wharncliffe-style John Jones damascus blade and a 416 stainless steel handle engraved by Jody Mueller.

In December 1998, MIKE PELLEGRIN and his granddaughter, Megan, were looking for something to do. Mike saw an ad for the St. Louis Gateway Knife Show and decided to go. Inside the show, he experienced the beauty of handmade knives for the first time in his life.

"Megan fell in love with a pearl-handle Lady Leg folder that had already been sold," Pellegrin remembers. "With the confidence every granddaughter has in her grandfather, she said I could make her one. Well, between her and Paul Myer, the maker of the Lady Leg, they convinced me that with Paul's help and guidance, and a lot of practice, I could make her a knife. This was despite the fact that, until that point in my life, my Victorinox knife, which I used to open mail and boxes, was all I knew about knives. My profession was barbering and the sales of barber and beauty supplies.

"I can't explain how lucky I was that the Lady Leg folder belonged to Paul Myer, one of the nicest, most patient and knowledgeable knifemakers I've met, and a great teacher as well. Even though I have never run out of questions, Paul and other knifemakers have always been generous with their help in answering them," Pellegrin relates.

His latest thrill was in January 2006 when he won the "Best In Show" award at the St. Louis Gateway Knife Show—the show that started him on the knifemaking path—for his Jurassic Night folder.

Equally stunning are the Daniel Ehrenberger damascus blade and the Turritella agate handle of Mike Pellegrin's lock-back folder. Turritella agate is from a sedimentary layer of earth that contains fossil shells of gastropods, small spiral-shelled prehistoric sea creatures. In keeping with the seashell theme, Pellegrin filed the bolsters into shell patterns in front and back.

Having proudly served in the U.S. Army 101st Airborne Division, MICHAEL TYRE had two tours in Vietnam under his belt before returning home a disabled veteran. He attended the University of Wisconsin where he majored in art, and attended a knife show in Mesa, Arizona, where he met knifemaker D' Alton Holder.

"D' Alton opened his shop to me and took the time to explain why you do certain things to make a quality knife," Tyre says. "I have gained so much knowledge and so many friendships from all the knifemakers I have met.

"I spent the time necessary in the shop with legendary Texas knifemaker Johnny Stout to learn the correct methods of fabricating quality locking-liner folders," Tyre continues. "His expert advice and instruction show in each knife I build."

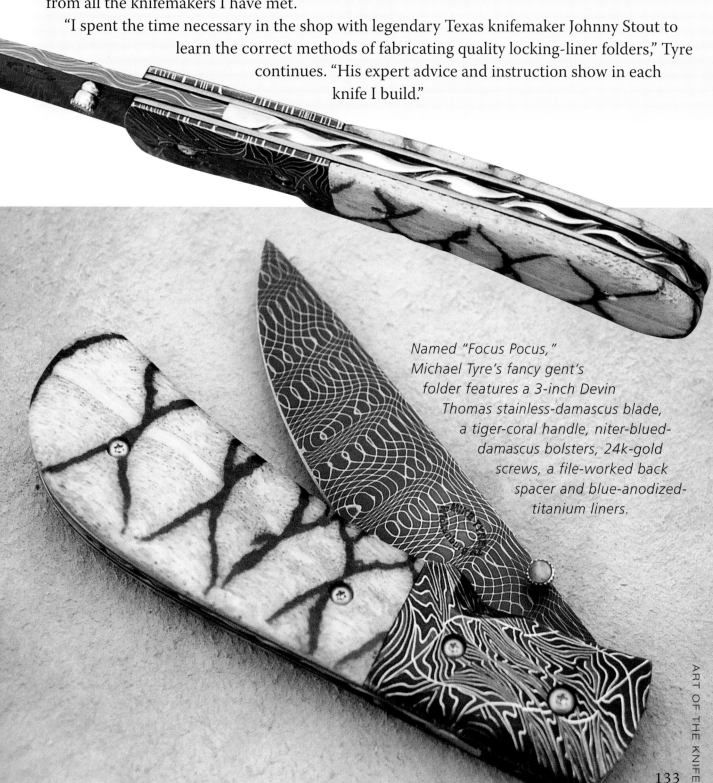

Named "Focus Pocus," Michael Tyre's fancy gent's folder features a 3-inch Devin Thomas stainless-damascus blade, a tiger-coral handle, niter-blued-damascus bolsters, 24k-gold screws, a file-worked back spacer and blue-anodized-titanium liners.

Left: Mammoth tooth is a handle material that has made inroads into the knife industry in the last couple years. Just adding mammoth tooth to an average folding knife does not make it a piece of art, however. Murray Sterling's locking-liner folder became an art form with the addition of a Robert Eggerling heat-colored damascus blade and bolsters, Murray's fancy file work along the inside liners, and his incredible fit and finish throughout the piece. **(Murray Sterling photo)**

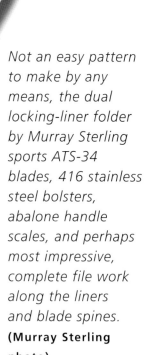

Not an easy pattern to make by any means, the dual locking-liner folder by Murray Sterling sports ATS-34 blades, 416 stainless steel bolsters, abalone handle scales, and perhaps most impressive, complete file work along the liners and blade spines. **(Murray Sterling photo)**

Above: *When you make knives as well as Howard Viele does, you tend to have connections. All three folders lock open via a Ball Lock™ that Howard licensed from Spyderco. The top knife, the "Push," is a Liong Mah design, while the bottom two models are all "Howard." Each showcases an ivory-Micarta® handle, a titanium frame and either a CPM S30V or Damasteel (center) blade.* **(PointSeven photo)**

Opposite page: *For his symmetrical folding dagger, the late Jim Schmidt made strikingly beautiful use of a mother-of-pearl handle, a clamshell-shaped gold lock-back mechanism, a sculpted mother-of-pearl thumb disc, and a damascus blade and bolsters.* **(Francesco Pachi photo)**

Using a similar anodized-titanium handle frame to his "Damascus Taboo" knife (below), Ken Onion changes the handle scheme, using a mammoth-ivory handle insert for his "Zero Tolerance" prototype. The knife also sports a damascus blade and a thumb stud fashioned by Jeff Park. **(Mitch Lum photo)**

The color scheme and damascus work on Ken Onion's "Damascus Taboo" knife are remarkable. The dark-black-and-gray damascus blade look is carried out throughout the anodized-titanium handle frame via puzzle-piece inlays. **(Mitch Lum photo)**

Richard Wright says he tends to be influenced by the Old World look and quality craftsmanship that came from the European styles of the late 1800s, as well as from some Sheffield folding bowies and older classic designs from Europe and America. His gold-lip-pearl-handle, damascus auto with fileworked back spacer, carved double guard and rear bolsters can trace its roots to elements of classic design. **(SharpByCoop.com photo)**

RICHARD WRIGHT'S background includes working as a gunsmith, welder, machinist and toolmaker. He began making knives when he was a boy, but never became serious about it until he made his first switchblade in 1991. "I find the mechanical intricacies and the 'forbidden fruit' aspect of automatic knives to be the focal point of what I enjoy about making them," he says. "I try not to make any two knives identical but will occasionally make several variations of a particular design."

The tight, lace-pattern mosaic-damascus blade and bolsters of Don Hanson III's folder butt up against a premium, presentation-grade, blue-Siberian-bark-mammoth-ivory handle, and the result is quite a striking knife. Though it looks like a traditional sunfish pattern, it's actually a locking-liner folder replete with mother-of-pearl inlays along the back spacer of the knife (inset top, right), an 18k-gold thumb stud and file-worked titanium liners. (SharpByCoop.com photo)

Kelly Carlson matched the caramel-colored mammoth-ivory handle of his "Icicle & Toothpick" folder with the copper-niobium bolsters. He anodized the titanium liners and back spacer to complement the hues, as well, and satin-finished a 3-inch D-2 blade, adding a 14k-gold thumb stud.

The blending of Damasteel stainless damascus and white mother-of-pearl was a stroke of genius by knifemaker Kevin Hoffman, with one material seemingly flowing into the other.

The Mediterranean red coral of Kevin Hoffman's folding knife could put the "red back into the sea," so to speak, and is complemented by a Damasteel stainless damascus blade and bolsters, all flawlessly executed.

In obtaining his Master of Arts degree in metal smithing and jewelry making from the University of Iowa, KEVIN HOFFMAN started to experiment with knives during his last semester of school. "My thesis included the making of several knives, as well as some jewelry, a sterling silver teapot and other functional and sculptural objects," he says. "Upon graduation, I had lost interest in making teapots and the idea of becoming a knifemaker took hold."

The tightly patterned blade and bolsters of Pat and Wes Crawford's "Perfigo" model are further enhanced by the natural character of the wooly-mammoth-tooth handle. The knife is photographed by PointSeven Studios on a wooly mammoth tooth.

It's tough to tear one's eyes away from the blue, purple, gold and beige wooly-mammoth-tooth handle of Pat and Wes Crawford's "Kasper" folder long enough to look at the damascus blade and bolsters. A Spyderco-style hole in the blade aids in easy one-hand opening, and other features include a file-worked back spacer, pocket clip and anodized-titanium liners. **(SharpByCoop.com photo)**

Kelly Carlson planted copper-color flowers between the creamy mammoth-ivory handle and steely D-2 blade of his fancy art folder. Delbert Ealy originally forged the damascus bolsters, which Carlson has since etched and heat colored. That's a sapphire set into the thumb stud.

Kelly Carlson hand finished the copper-niobium handle of his "Icicle" folder using polymer ceramic materials similar to those employed by dentists for repairing teeth.

Following the shaping of the copper niobium handle, he etched it to relieve the copper component from the niobium ovals, and then undercut it using engraving tools to facilitate a good mechanical bond with the ceramic inlays.

Carlson applied the polymer ceramic material, in this case colored green, in multiple layers until level with the niobium and providing the desired depth of color, with each coat fully cured by application of specialized U/V light, again similar to dental tools. Following the final curing, he sands and polishes the excess polymer ceramic to expose the niobium ovals for anodizing to provide a bright, gold color.

The handle is matched perfectly with a tightly patterned Mike Norris damascus blade and a 14k-gold thumb stud.

Made for actor Steven Segal, the "Samurai Habu" is a Ken Onion frame-lock folder with a handle fully engraved by C.J. Cai, and a sweet, re-curved CPM S30V blade. (Mitch Lum photo)

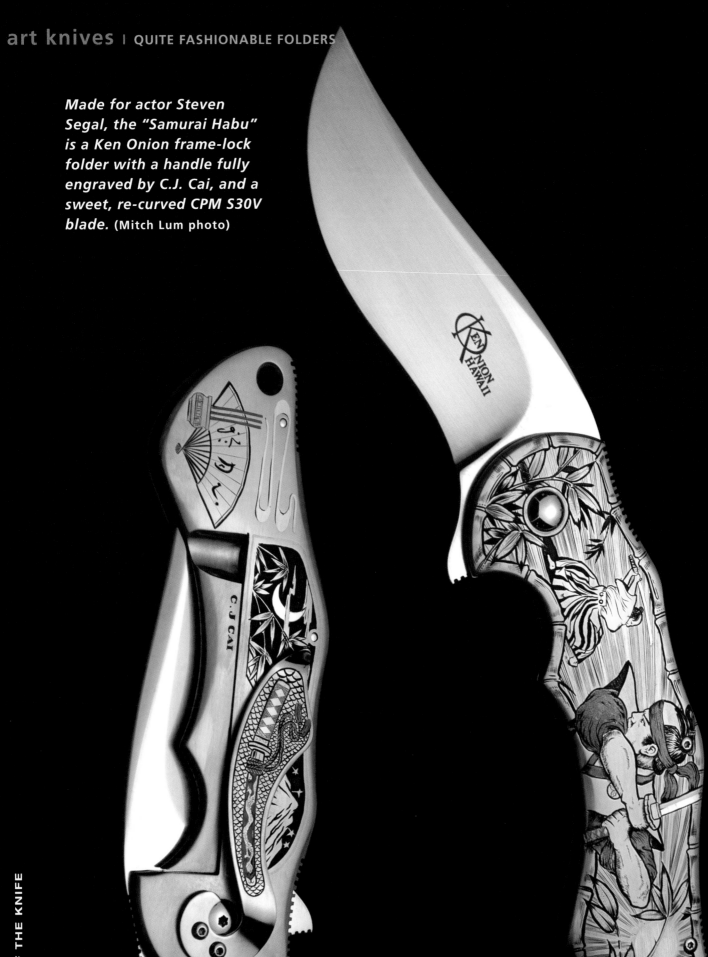

The dye job on the box-elder-burl handle of Scot Matsuoka's curvaceous cutter would make even the least vain of fashion models jealous. The fashionable folder also sports a CPM 154CM blade and titanium bolsters. **(PointSeven photo)**

The way the cloth was woven before compressed to make the G-10 handle is why it is called a "silver twill" G-10 grip, and just as detailed is the sharp, wavy CPM 154CM blade. Scot Matsuoka's 8-inch folder, which looks like it could cut in several directions, also features titanium bolsters. **(PointSeven photo)**

Steve Johnson etched the words "My first folder S.R. Johnson 1994-2001" on the blade of his shapely, pearl-handle, locking-liner folding knife. **(PointSeven photo)**

Opposite page: Richard Hehn cut a swath across the mammoth-ivory handle of his integral folder, giving the hot little slicing machine a slinky look and feel. **(Francesco Pachi photo)**

NORMAN E. SANDOW

Below: *Walrus tooth is the centerpiece of Norman Sandow's locking-liner folder, a jaw-dropping find from the Antarctic and estimated to be over 300 years old. The hand-rubbed ATS-34 blade is a bit more modern, as are the bead-blasted titanium bolsters and jeweled liners. Mother-of-pearl set into the thumb stud is a nice finishing touch.*

Norman Sandow says there is "no sloppiness whatsoever" in the blade of this locking-liner folder, meaning it does not wiggle and exhibits "smooth action," signs of a properly centered and fitted blade. There is also no sloppiness in the fit and finish of the twist-pattern damascus and giraffe-bone handle. Maroon dye was dabbed onto the white giraffe bone slabs before they were buffed to obtain a speckled finish. The bolsters are mosaic damascus that Sandow acid etched, carded with steel wool, niter-colored and rubbed with fine abrasive paper.

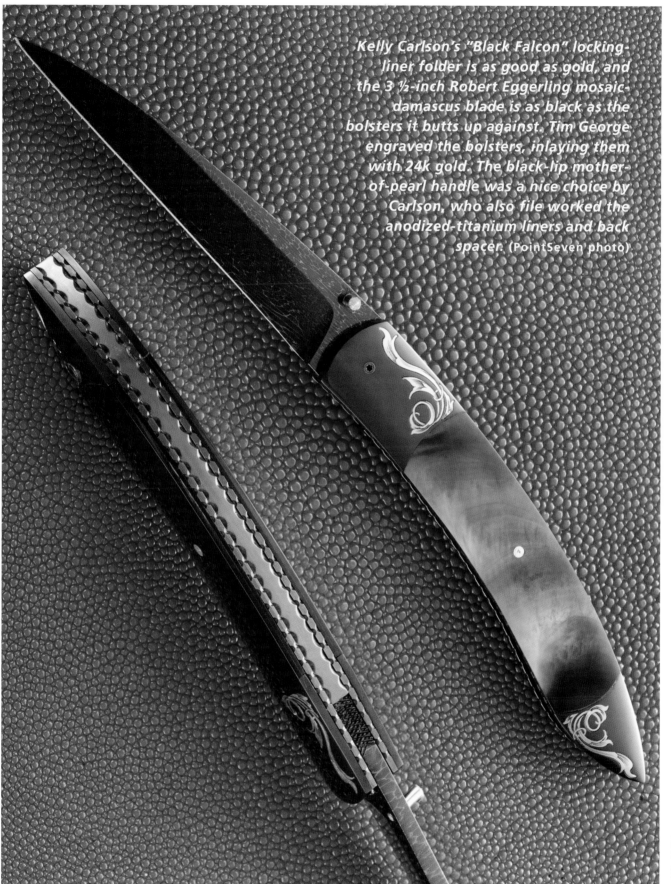

Kelly Carlson's "Black Falcon" locking-liner folder is as good as gold, and the 3 ½-inch Robert Eggerling mosaic-damascus blade is as black as the bolsters it butts up against. Tim George engraved the bolsters, inlaying them with 24k gold. The black-lip mother-of-pearl handle was a nice choice by Carlson, who also file worked the anodized-titanium liners and back spacer. (PointSeven photo)

Did someone say "geometric?" Meet Germany's own Jurgen Steinau, the master at making knives into geometric works of art, and in this case in the architectural style of the 1920s Art Deco period. The fantastic set of two Art Deco knives are from the collection of Pierluigi Peroni.
(Francesco Pachi photo)

There aren't many material goods in the world worth having more than a Jim Schmidt inter-frame dagger with premium black-lip mother-of-pearl handle inlays, gold liners and a gold bail on the back of the handle. Mr. Schmidt passed away years ago, but Pierluigi Peroni is the knife collector with the coveted goods. (Francesco Pachi photo)

IN THE BEST OF BOWIE TRADITIONS

A small bowie, measuring just 11 ½ inches overall, Mike Ruth's damascus and stag sticker packs a powerful punch. **(Ward photo)**

The *"Red River Bowie" was fashioned by Mike Williams using a 5160-and-15N20-damascus blade, a stag handle and heat-colored stainless steel fittings.*

(Ward photo)

Among the many lines of the Gaetan Beauchamp bowie knife are those of the swooping clip-point blade, the Swedish stainless damascus, the mammoth-molar-tooth handle and the file-worked guard.
(Alain Miville-Deschenes photo)

ROBERT BLASINGAME began making knives in the early 1960s while working for a farm equipment manufacturer in West Texas. "The company had a blacksmith shop and the blacksmith, Nealie Hightower, taught me to forge 'corn knives' from steel cable," Blasingame remembers. "In 1985 I built my shop and smithy where I undertook full-time knifemaking."

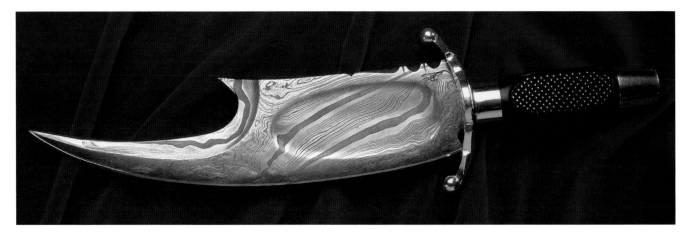

Robert Blasingame specializes in fashioning antique bowie reproductions and slip-joint folders. He is a member of the Texas Knifemakers and Collectors Association and the American Bladesmith Society. The "Damsel of Deguello" model is a commissioned fantasy bowie with an 11 ½-inch, hammer-forged twist-pattern-damascus blade. The radical clip-point blade is hollow ground and features a file-worked spine. The fittings are mild steel and the handle is African blackwood with four raised, checkered panels and silver pins. It took two years to complete the piece.

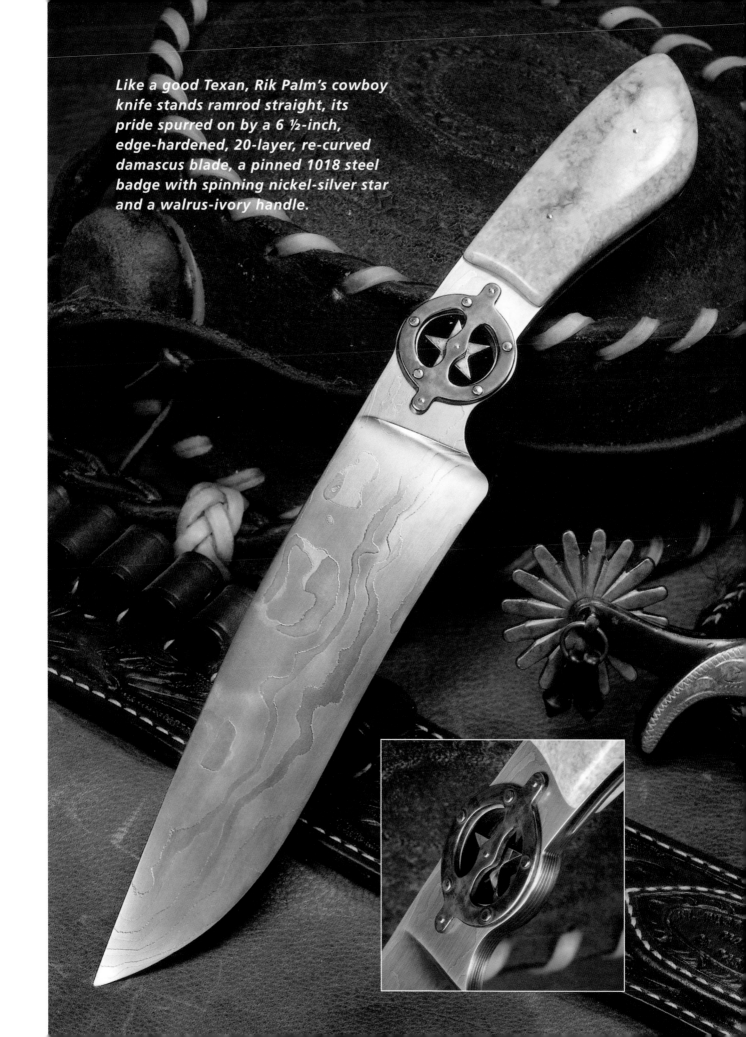

Like a good Texan, Rik Palm's cowboy knife stands ramrod straight, its pride spurred on by a 6 ½-inch, edge-hardened, 20-layer, re-curved damascus blade, a pinned 1018 steel badge with spinning nickel-silver star and a walrus-ivory handle.

Fred Rowe made the bowie as a tribute to his son, who is in the Air Force. The colors and style were chosen to complement the new Air Force uniforms. Most notable are the blue spacers that were sliced from a bowling ball. A stabilized and dyed box-elder-burl handle fits the color scheme, and other features include a forged wrought-iron guard with a torch-blued finish, a clay-hardened 1080 blade, a 410 stainless steel butt cap, and black and blue fiber spacers. **(U.S. Air Force photo of soldier in uniform by Master Sgt. Jim Varhegyi)**

FRED ROWE says his original knife designs come from the "form follows function" school of design. His main focus is on bowies and hunters with intricate and unusual handles. "I consider all 'stable' materials for possible inclusion in the knives I make. One example is the slices of a beautiful blue bowling ball that were included in the knife shown here," he notes. "It was one material I found that had the proper colors and tone required." All knives from Rowe's forge are of "sole authorship" construction, meaning he completed each step of the knifemaking process himself.

Sixteen stainless steel pins hold the mastodon ivory handle onto the full tang of Steven Koster's 5160 bowie. Rope file work garnishes the nickel silver guard. Koster also hand-stitched the leather sheath.

"My anvil was salvaged out of a lake in northern Idaho and my forge is a shop-built unit that measures 12 inches in vertical diameter and is force fed with propane and air," knifemaker STEVEN KOSTER explains. "I use a 5-inch vertical ram press for damascus."

Koster fashions only five-to-10 knives per year and tries to keep most of his pieces in the $200-$800 range. "I use mostly natural handle materials, including stag, fossil ivory and bone, various woods and leather," he notes. "I also make my own sheaths, some to match the handles, and I include silver tips and throats on bowie and dagger sheaths."

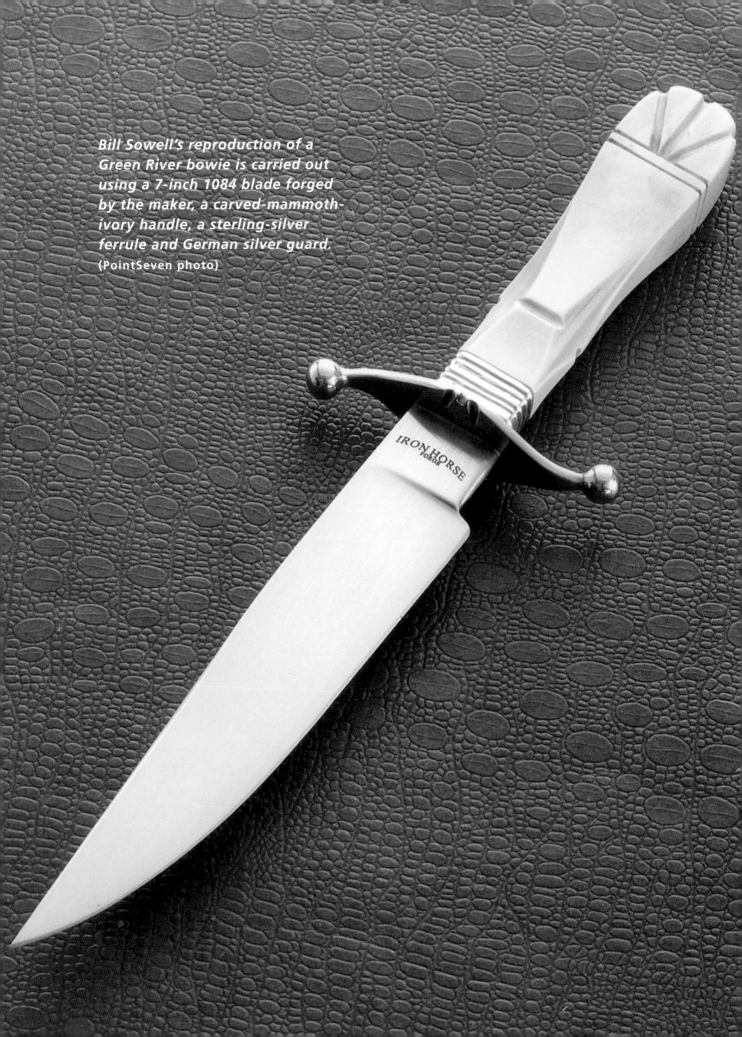

Bill Sowell's reproduction of a Green River bowie is carried out using a 7-inch 1084 blade forged by the maker, a carved-mammoth-ivory handle, a sterling-silver ferrule and German silver guard. (PointSeven photo)

Art often reveals itself in simplicity of form and function, and such is the case with the impeccably fit and finished bowie by Bill Sowell of Iron Horse Forge. Exacting details include a hand-forged 5160 blade, a desert-ironwood handle and 416 stainless steel fittings. Sowell also fashioned a sharkskin sheath for the piece. **(Hoffman photo)**

The coffin handle, named for its shape, of Bill Sowell's vest bowie, named for where such pieces were traditionally worn, is ebony with a nickel-silver shield. It accompanies a hand-forged 1084 blade, 416 stainless steel fittings and a crocodile-skin sheath. **(Hoffman photo)**

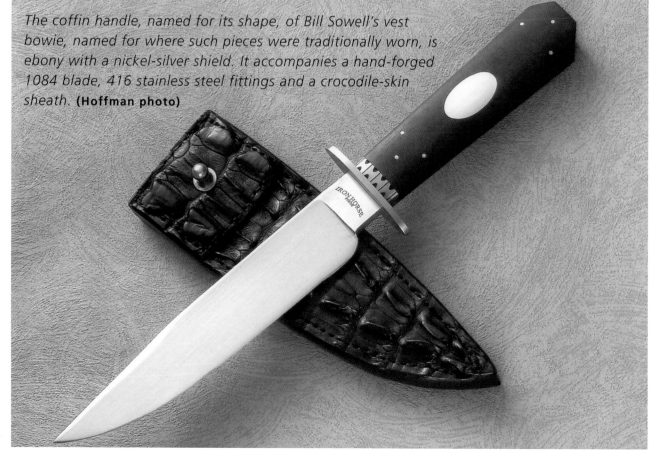

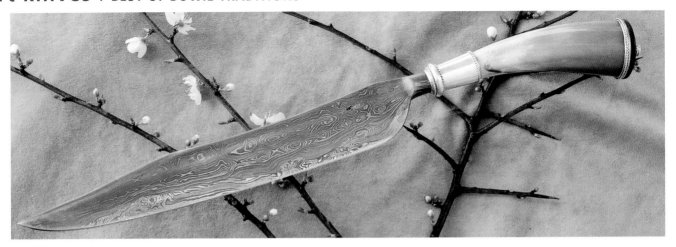

The six-bar-damascus blade of Richard van Dijk's integral bowie stretches 9 inches and is complemented by a New Zealand cow-horn handle capped with sterling silver fittings and a damascus pommel.

Knifemaker RICHARD VAN DIJK lives and works on the Otago Peninsula near Dunedin, New Zealand, and his trademark business name is Hoiho Knives. "Hoiho" is the Maori name for the rarest penguin in the world, the yellow-eyed penguin, that lives and breeds along the coasts of the Otago Peninsula.

Born and raised in the Netherlands, van Dijk trained as a goldsmith at Schoonhoven. In 1971, he spent a year traveling in New Zealand and made up his mind to go back. He immigrated to New Zealand in 1979 and has been employed as a goldsmith there.

"In 1995, I met a blacksmith who introduced me to forge welding [forging damascus blade steel], and I got the bug. I have made mainly damascus knives since," van Dijk says. "I tend to use my jewelry skills in knifemaking, preferring to employ natural handle materials and fashion fixed-blade knives."

The Richard van Dijk bowie dons a 320-layer damascus blade. "The pattern was made by cutting the blade billet diagonally, turning the two halves around, and welding them back together again," van Dijk explains. The knife also sports a New Zealand deer-antler handle impregnated with mineral oil and capped with brass fittings.

Not only are the engraved guard and pommel of the Pedro Gibert bowie noteworthy, but their shape, form and harmonic relationship to the overall knife pattern are significant. The red liner placed between stag handle slabs is a detail that only trained eyes catch.

The details of the Pedro Gibert elephant-ivory-handle bowie are in its file-worked guard, engraved bolster and pommel, embroidered and hand stitched leather sheath and carved beech-wood box.

Don Hanson III's S-Guard Bowie/Fighter stretches 14 ½ inches long, including a 9 ½-inch, 500-layer, random-pattern-damascus blade. The handle is premium fossil-walrus-tusk ivory, and copper spacers complement the wrought iron S-guard. There is one 18k-gold pin in the handle. (SharpByCoop.com photo)

DON HANSON III was in the commercial deep-sea-fishing business in the 1980s, and one of the first knives he made was a bait-cutting knife. "It is now being used in my kitchen to cut up veggies," he says. "Just recently, I have started making forged bowies and fixed blades with traditional damascus and high-carbon-steel blades, the latter including vivid hamons, or temper lines.

"I began forging my own damascus in 1994, starting out with trips to the National Ornamental Metals Museum in Memphis, Tenn.," Hanson adds. "With help from my Memphis friends, I was able to forge my first damascus."

ART OF THE KNIFE

The re-curved blade and fancy file work along the spine of Wolfgang Dell's bowie give it a curvaceous look, as well as the cutting power of a sickle. Dell deep-cooled the 4192 blade, butting it up against a white-as-a-ghost walrus-tusk handle and a damascus cross-guard.

"Since I made my first knife, this intensive hobby has become an experience that I'd never imagined," says German knifemaker WOLFGANG DELL. "As a result of the numerous domestic and international knife shows I have visited, as well as being published in various magazines, many knife collectors have become aware of my work. Meanwhile my clients are international. I have customers in Australia, Mexico, the United States, Switzerland, France, Italy and Germany who have contributed to my growing success."

An acorn shield classily adorns the ebony grip of Wolfgang Dell's clean, impressive bowie.

"On the occasion of a paddle trip in Alaska, I was looking for a fairly big knife, preferably in the shape of a bowie," remembers knifemaker Wolfgang Dell. "I was unable to find something reasonable. Therefore, I made my own knife. It was big, and heavy, too, and I still like it today."

Ernie Grospitch says that the knife and sheath work are done by him, "warts and all," in his shop. "Nothing are farmed out," he notes. There aren't many warts on the Bowie Number 1 model that exhibits a 10 ½-inch, convex-ground D-2 blade, a wooly-mammoth-tooth handle with mammoth-ivory spacers and a brass guard. The leather sheath is embellished with a handcrafted arrowhead on the toe section, a squirrel-pelt belt and an antique belt buckle.

Hand forged by Robert Blasingame, the 9 ¼-inch blade of his Bart Moore reproduction bowie is in the San Mai style, including L-6 high-carbon steel sandwiched between layers of chain-saw damascus. Other amenities include an oak handle, and a fire-blued, mild-steel guard and fittings.

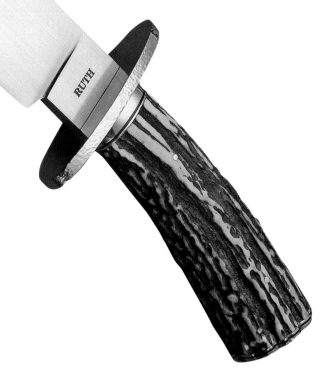

Using only three ingredients—stag for the handle, 5160 blade steel and a stainless steel guard—journeyman smith Mike Ruth built a flawless bowie knife. **(Ward photo)**

Above: *The 9 ¼-inch 5160 blade of Lin Rhea's "Boone's Lick Bowie" measures 1 ½ inches from edge to spine and is complemented by a desert-ironwood grip. "I think the length, width and other characteristics of the blade fit the ratios that are necessary for it to look right," he says.* **(Ward photo)**

Before the hunt, native Plains Indians would have a prayer ceremony asking The Creator to bless the hunt, and make it fruitful and safe. A typical ceremonial pipe was fashioned from pipestone (Catlinite) mined from what is now the Pipestone National Monument in Southwest Minnesota. Native peoples have mined that deposit for hundreds of years. Pipestone was considered a sacred stone, and hence the reason for the pipestone in the knife handle and blade of ED BRANDSEY'S custom bowie (right).

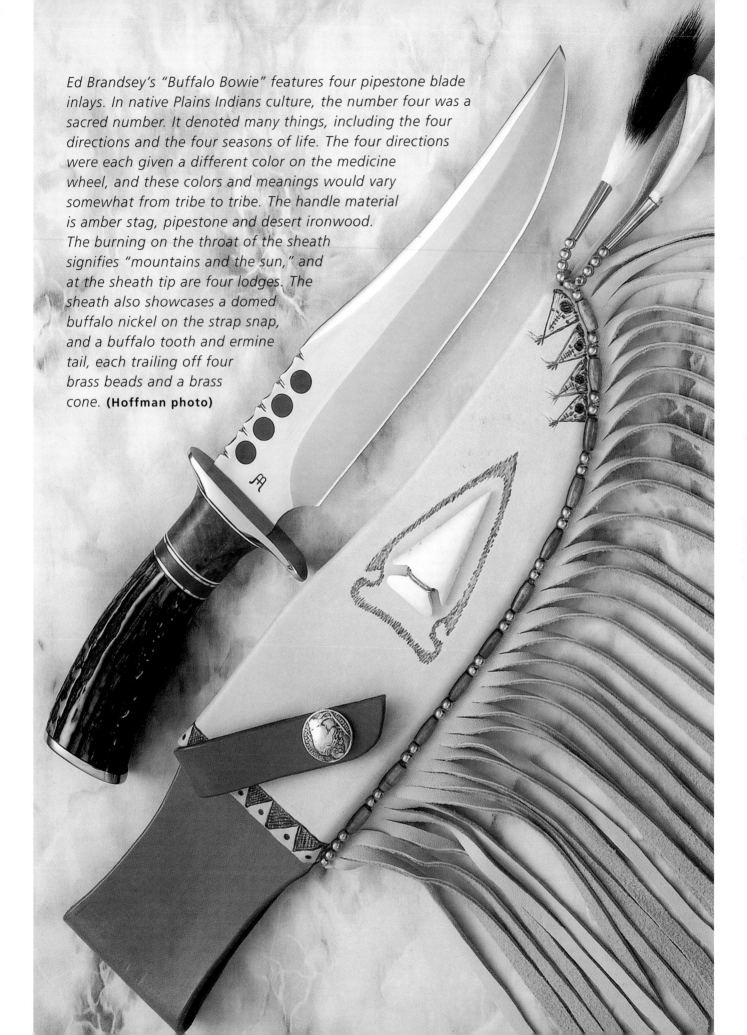

Ed Brandsey's "Buffalo Bowie" features four pipestone blade inlays. In native Plains Indians culture, the number four was a sacred number. It denoted many things, including the four directions and the four seasons of life. The four directions were each given a different color on the medicine wheel, and these colors and meanings would vary somewhat from tribe to tribe. The handle material is amber stag, pipestone and desert ironwood. The burning on the throat of the sheath signifies "mountains and the sun," and at the sheath tip are four lodges. The sheath also showcases a domed buffalo nickel on the strap snap, and a buffalo tooth and ermine tail, each trailing off four brass beads and a brass cone. **(Hoffman photo)**

THE DARING
DANCE OF
DAMASCUS

The singular combination of "carbodium" damascus and tiger coral turns Francesco Pachi's small tanto into a gargantuan work of art. (Pachi photo)

Left: *The Swedish stainless damascus of Gaetan Beauchamp's dagger incorporates a tight pattern in places, a non-distinct pattern in others and brightly etched splotches here and there, almost natural looking, as with the appearance of the mammoth-molar-tooth handle.* **(Alain Miville-Deschenes photo)**

Below: *Ten inches of Devin Thomas damascus patterning spread across the blade of Frank Gamble's bowie as if they are water washing down a car window. A file-worked gold guard and mother-of-pearl handle complete the piece.* **(Stanley Chan photo)**

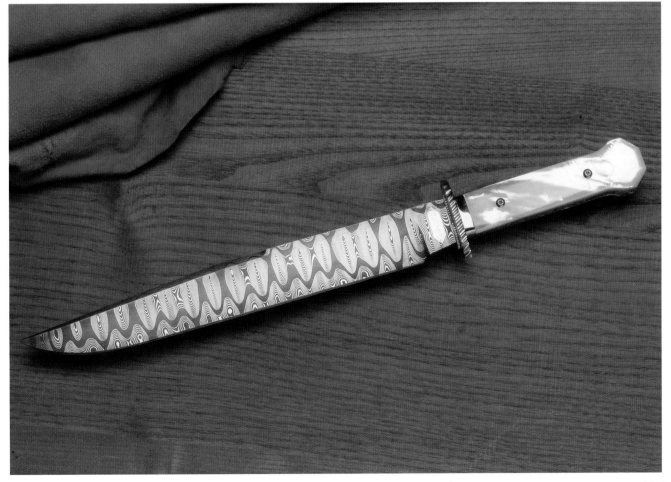

George Werth forged the damascus blade, guard and butt cap of Michael Kanter's "Revolver," but Kanter gave it the blue finish, accessorizing it with an amber-colored stag handle, a mammoth-tooth section, and titanium and copper spacers. The knife can be completely disassembled by unscrewing the nut at the back of the handle.

MICHAEL KANTER'S business name is Adam Michael Knives. "I started making knives in 2000 when my son, Adam, was two years old. The first knife I made was engraved with his name on it [Adam Michael], and the business name just stuck," Kanter explains.

"All of my knives are completely handmade and hand ground without the use of fixtures. I use no prefabricated parts in the construction except for the occasional mosaic pin," he notes. "I take great pride in the quality of my knives and I strive to make the next knife better than the previous one."

Opposite page: *Loyd W. Thomsen forged three kinds of damascus for the same knife, including a twisted, fire-blued guard, a kaleidoscope-pattern butt cap and lanyard ring, and a fireball-pattern blade. Thomsen split the foot-long blade billet horizontally and forged it back together before giving it a fashionable flat grind. The handle is exhibition-grade elk antler.* **(Jennifer Connell photo, JCDesign@Rushmore.com)**

"*My interest in knives began at 8 years old, but the film* **The Iron Mistress** *was my real inspiration,"* Australian knifemaker Joe Zemitis says. *"The first knife I made was a bowie from spring steel with an oak handle."* The bowie-style fixed blade showcases a W-1, wrought iron and pure-nickel-damascus blade, 416 stainless steel bolsters and an antique-elephant-ivory handle scrimshawed by Zemitis's wife, Jolanta.

Joe Zemitis wrestled W-1 and W-2 steels, wrought iron and pure nickel into a ladder-pattern-damascus dagger blade, complementing it with a 416 stainless steel guard inset with a garnet, and a whale-ivory and oosic handle. The pommel is titanium, sterling silver and amber. The Osage-orange-wood sheath sports a nickel-silver throat and tip, and an inset of amber topped off with a carved-sterling-silver flower.

Perhaps it is the way Bill Coffey hot-blued the crossroads-pattern Robert Eggerling damascus blade and bolsters, or maybe it is the way he dyed the giraffe-bone handle blue and white, but somehow the knife has an icy look and feel to it that is nothing short of appealing. Coffey fully file-worked the titanium liners and damascus back spacer, anodizing them blue.

Above: *Michael Zscherny's early years of knifemaking consisted of fashioning hunters, boot knives and daggers. Since he enjoys the challenge of the mechanical properties of folding knives, he's focused all of his attention lately on folders. In the art-folder genre are two damascus pieces, one with a Robert Eggerling damascus blade and bolsters (top) and one with a Mike Norris ladder-pattern stainless damascus blade and Eggerling mosaic-damascus bolsters. Zscherny smartly heat treated the bolsters and married them with complementary mammoth-ivory (top) and carved black-lip-pearl handles. Diamonds grace the gold thumb studs.*

Left: *Austrian knifemaker Johannes Ebner has been forging damascus blades since 1990. The blade of his bowie is three-bar twist damascus forged together with elements of mosaic damascus and married with a Turkish-damascus guard and pommel. The handle material of choice is a slab of highly figured mammoth ivory with just the right crackled appearance.*

The herringbone-like lines of the Daryl Meier Turkish-twist damascus enliven Bud Nealy's "Coulter's Camp Knife." The piece also sports a Sambar-stag handle, mosaic pins and Turkish-twist-pattern damascus bolsters.

Doing the damascus dance on a bowie blade is Johannes Ebner who forged mosaic damascus together with three bars of twist damascus. The blade collar is nickel silver, the guard a twist damascus and the handle oosic.

Forging pictures in steel has become an art form that several knifemakers have undertaken over the past several years. None are better at it than Cliff Parker, who went as far as forging a complete sea theme into the blade of a black-pearl-handle folder. Taking center stage in the blade steel are sea snails, crabs, clams, conk shells, starfish, dolphins, sharks and pinwheels. (PointSeven photo)

Those who forge damascus steel, the people who take it upon themselves to study the edge geometry of knife blades, experts in all aspects of cutting, tend to like the tight damascus patterns, though not always. In the case of Don Hethcoat's exceptional folder, the tight damascus blade pattern is interrupted by wide whirlpool-like swaths, complemented by radial-pattern damascus bolsters and soothed by the translucent beauty of a mother-of-pearl handle.
(Weyer photo)

Below: Blade smith Don Hethcoat achieved the blade pattern by utilizing powder-steel technology, the art of forging powder metals together to create patterns. Usually the blade patterns are carefully planned, but at other times the patterning is a surprise to the smith after the blade is etched. Don knew what to do with the steel once he had it, marrying it with a radial-pattern-damascus guard, a stag handle and a showcase-ready Alvin Chewiwi leather sheath embellished with the artist's rendition of a buffalo head. (Hoffman photo)

George Baartman's "Purple People Eaters" (the author's name for them) feature mosaic-damascus bolsters forged by, from top, Ettore Gianferrari, Joel Davis and Chris Mark. Yet it's the purplish treatment, or rather heat-treat, of the damascus that takes Baartman's locking-liner folders to the level of hot handcrafting. Each is married with natural handle materials, including, from top, desert ironwood, mammoth ivory and mother-of-pearl. Robert Eggerling forged the bottom blade, while the other two are Damasteel damascus.

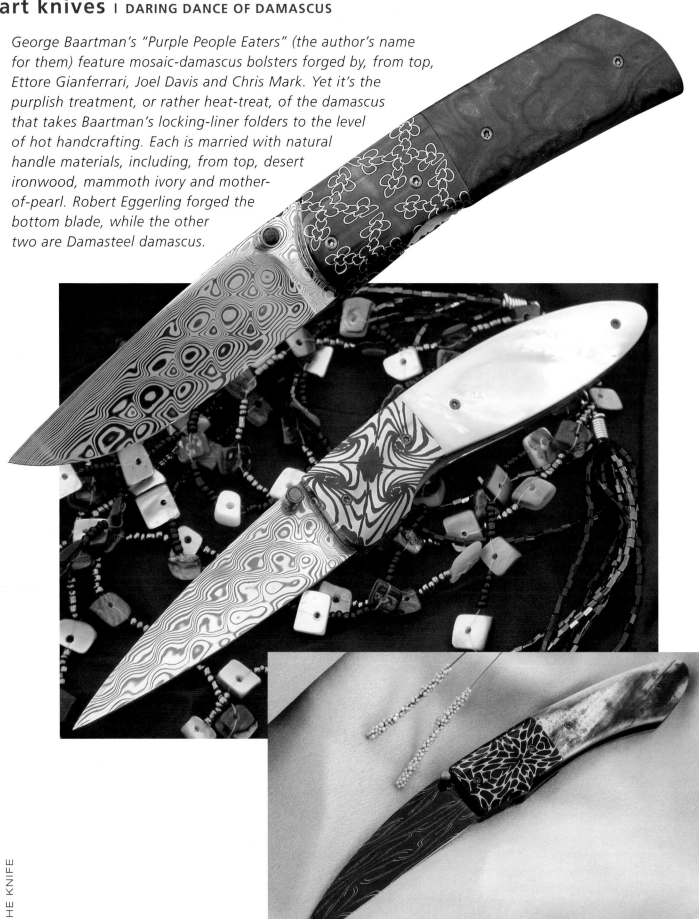

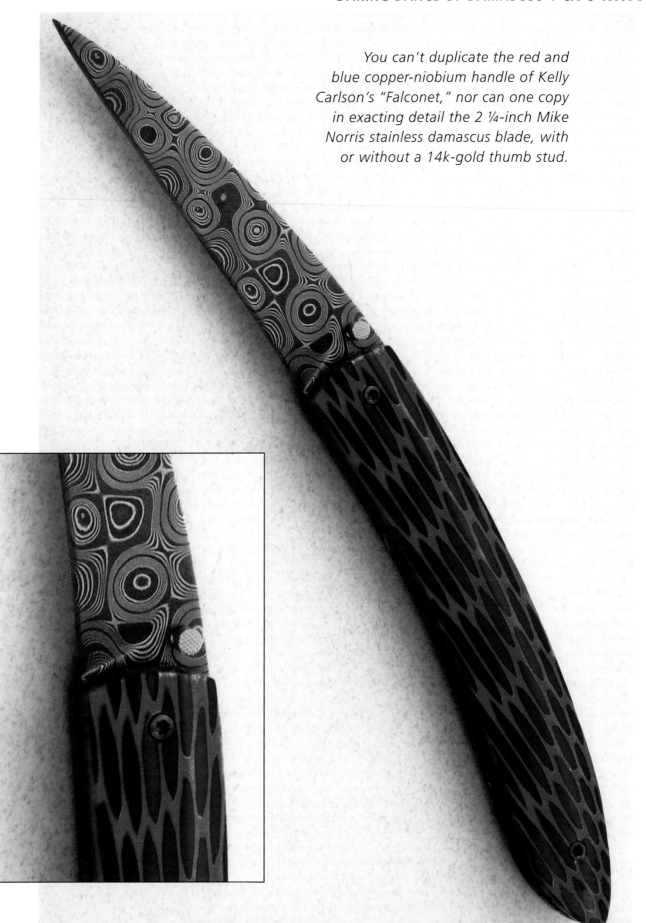

You can't duplicate the red and blue copper-niobium handle of Kelly Carlson's "Falconet," nor can one copy in exacting detail the 2 ¼-inch Mike Norris stainless damascus blade, with or without a 14k-gold thumb stud.

The lines, circles and waves of the Mike Norris stainless damascus literally skip along the knife blade, yet the steel is not all about aesthetics. The core of the blade is 90 percent CPM S30V, making it a cutting machine. The Jim Harrison folder also features a damascus pocket clip and bolsters, titanium liners and a mammoth-ivory grip.

"I have a master's degree in industrial design, which has helped me in refining my knife designs," notes JENS ANSO. "After graduating, I decided to become a full-time knifemaker, and although it has been hard at times, I have never looked back with regret. I like being able to do what I enjoy the most and especially appreciate being my own boss.

"My workshop is my cave," he adds. "I love being in the shop surrounded by tools and materials."

Jens Anso's first double-action automatic knife sports a 5 ¾-inch, hollow-ground blade of Bertie Rietveld "dragon-skin-pattern" damascus. The heat-blued bolsters are Bjarne Rasmussen's "explosion-pattern" damascus, and the handle is 300-year-old sea cow bone. The firing button is fashioned from the same dragon-skin damascus as the blade.

A takedown model (the handle parts are removable), Lamont Coombs Jr.'s sub-hilt fighter features a Delbert Ealy tiger-pattern damascus blade and a walrus-ivory handle. Coombs also fashioned the leather sheath, adding white- and black-snakeskin inlays to accent the ivory knife handle. **(Rene Roy photo)**

Even though he makes a couple art knives each year, LAMONT COOMBS JR. says he concentrates on fashioning high-quality "using" knives. "I do all my own heat-treating for my blades, and I like to be able to control every aspect of making a blade myself. I have tested my knives and am confident in their performance," Coombs remarks. "I believe that, just as artful the knife design, so too should be the sheath design. The latter should 'flow' with the concept of the knife.

"I am still thirsty for knowledge and always try to keep an open mind about learning new things," Coombs continues. "I am planning to learn the art of engraving as a next step in my knifemaking evolution."

Opposite page: *Jens Anso made the matched hunting set for the gamekeeper of one of the largest Danish castles. The set consists of a folder and fixed blade, both equipped with hand-tooled leather sheaths, twist-pattern stainless-Damasteel blades and Siberian-mammoth-ivory handles.*

Don't let the cartoon-like character of the green sea snail fool you, the damascus blade can cut. Adding to the slapstick nature of the piece, knifemaker and blade forger Cliff Parker says he depicted what the snail looked like just before being knocked in the head and the shell taken from him. The gorgeous pearl grip does the knife justice. (PointSeven photo)

The "Six Guns for Seneca Sue" knife also showcases a mastodon-ivory handle, a 10 ½-inch spear-point blade with a semi-flat grind and a convex edge, and a file-worked silver guard. **(PointSeven photo)**

"Make him or break him, it is the duty of the smith to do his best to try and satisfy the requests of prospective customers," says RAYMOND RYBAR JR. "Each and every forged blade is special. Its reason for existence may not be fully realized by the forging smith, and possibly not even by the purchaser.

"Sue Amos is no greenhorn when it comes to the best in guns and knives. At the most recognized knife show in the world—the BLADE Show in Atlanta—Sue is always one of the first on the floor with an early-admission VIP pass, and she is consistently one of the last to leave. Sue understands the forging process from start to finish," Rybar adds. "She knows what she wants and what she doesn't want. This is both a blessing and a curse for the maker, depending on what they have to offer.

"Sue's dream blade was no easy matter," Rybar concludes. "She is a single-action pistol shooter, so mosaic pistols in the blade steel were a must. Along with the guns, the blade needed a 12 1/2-gallon cowboy hat, cowboy boots and spurs. She wanted "Seneca Sue" etched into the blade surface and, if possible, a favorite Bible verse—Psalm 23."

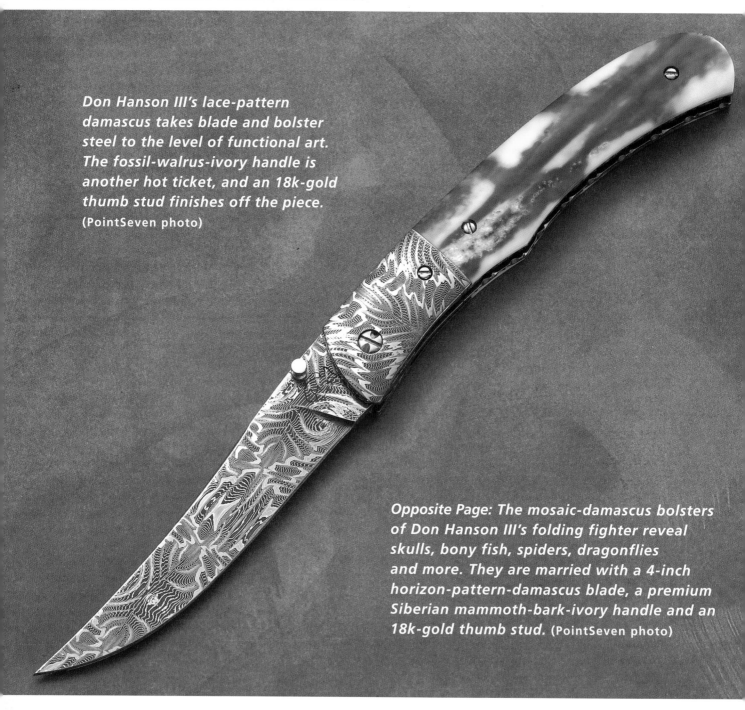

Don Hanson III's lace-pattern damascus takes blade and bolster steel to the level of functional art. The fossil-walrus-ivory handle is another hot ticket, and an 18k-gold thumb stud finishes off the piece. (PointSeven photo)

Opposite Page: The mosaic-damascus bolsters of Don Hanson III's folding fighter reveal skulls, bony fish, spiders, dragonflies and more. They are married with a 4-inch horizon-pattern-damascus blade, a premium Siberian mammoth-bark-ivory handle and an 18k-gold thumb stud. (PointSeven photo)

An American Bladesmith Society journeyman smith, DON HANSON III has enough room in his shop for two Little Giant power hammers—a 25-pound unit and a 100-pound hammer—and a forging area with two gas forges and a 24-ton press. "With this equipment, I am able to forge traditional damascus along with mosaic damascus for all my knives," Hanson says.

Four hundred layers of 1084 and 15N20 tool steel compose the 16-inch damascus blade of Wally Hayes's wakizashi. A silk-wrapped, black-stingray-skin handle and copper menuki (handle charm) complete the piece. It comes with Kydex® and nylon sheaths. **(PointSeven photo)**

"I recently produced some Japanese blades in true fashion—with 1,600 layers of carburized, electrolytic iron hardened in water," says American Bladesmith Society master smith WALLY HAYES. "And, after years of trying, I finally figured out how to get choji temper lines. The choji temper line is only produced when all the forging, hardening/tempering and quenching variables are correct, producing one of the most beautiful temper lines the Japanese ever created."

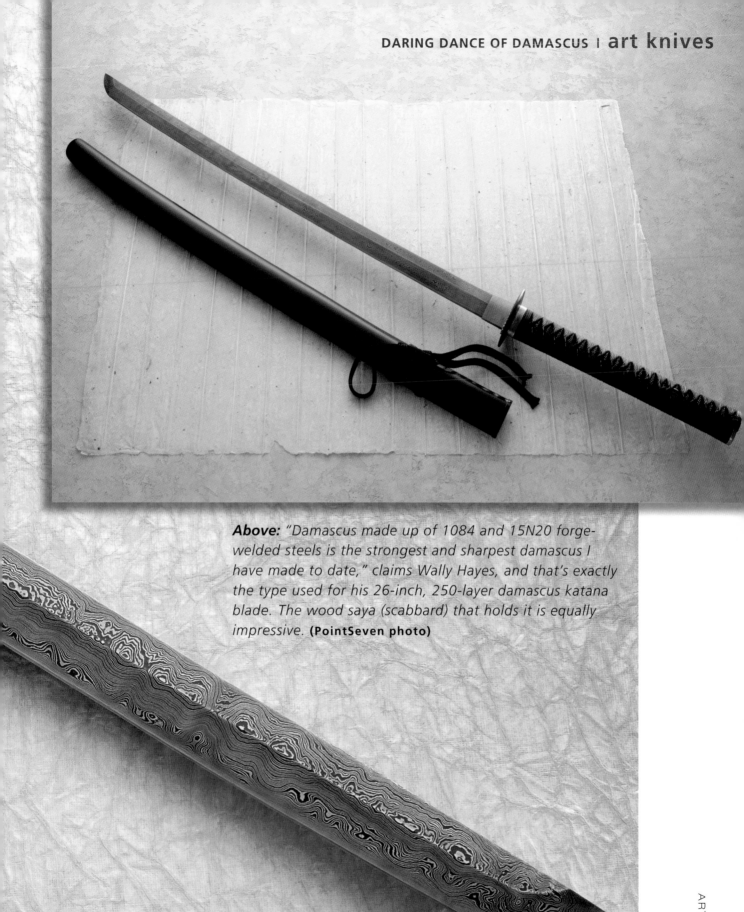

Above: "Damascus made up of 1084 and 15N20 forge-welded steels is the strongest and sharpest damascus I have made to date," claims Wally Hayes, and that's exactly the type used for his 26-inch, 250-layer damascus katana blade. The wood saya (scabbard) that holds it is equally impressive. **(PointSeven photo)**

The nickel-and-1095-damascus blade of Raymond Rybar Jr.'s art piece is fashioned in a bayonet style grind with a file-worked spine. After hardening and tempering the blade, Rybar etched and blued the steel. The curved semi-D-guard is blued steel, and the handle is ancient walrus ivory with a silver and steel file-worked butt. **(PointSeven photo)**

"At 58 years old, it is still quite vivid in my mind being mesmerized by blacksmiths and farriers bending and shaping hot iron and steel with relative ease while watching on as a youngster growing up 20 miles south of Pittsburgh, Pa.," recalls RAYMOND RYBAR JR.

"I eventually learned to shoe horses, and after my duty to service ended in 1971, I shod horses at a standard-bred racetrack not far from Pittsburgh until 1987," he adds. "In the winter most of the horses would leave for racetracks in warmer climates like Florida and California, and like many a horseshoer, I tinkered with forging knives, tomahawks, bear traps and any other iron or steel object of interest."

Opposite page: *To achieve a blade that tells part of the story of Adam and Eve, Raymond Rybar Jr. forged nickel and high-carbon damascus together with wrought iron, then twisted and forged them to give himself non-damascus plates. High carbon steel was added to the edges for hardening, tempering, sharpening and cutting. The pictures of Adam and Eve were etched with a 50/50 nitric and hydrochloric acid mix. The scriptural quotes were also etched. The file-worked guard is wrought iron, and the handle is a well-weathered branch from a huge, dead ironwood tree. The snake is solid silver.* **(PointSeven photo)**

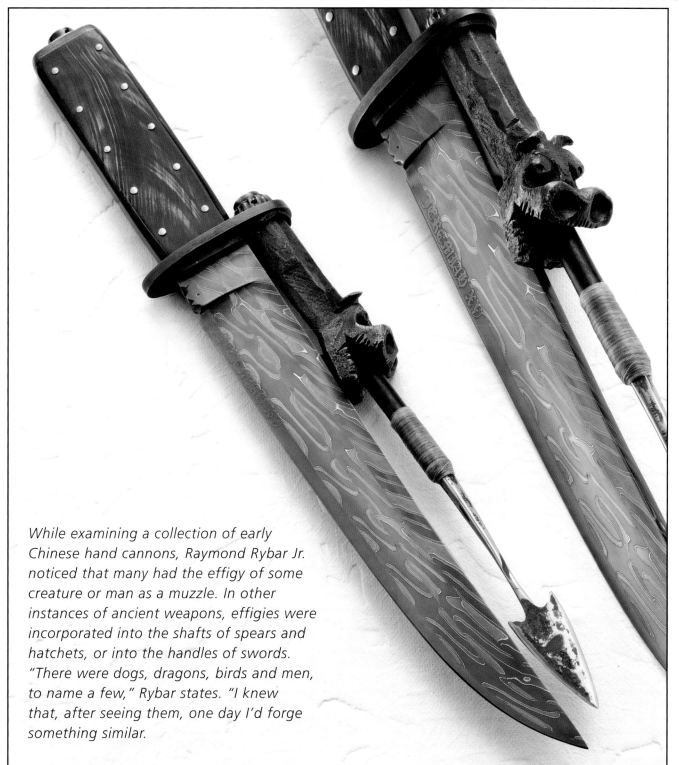

While examining a collection of early Chinese hand cannons, Raymond Rybar Jr. noticed that many had the effigy of some creature or man as a muzzle. In other instances of ancient weapons, effigies were incorporated into the shafts of spears and hatchets, or into the handles of swords. "There were dogs, dragons, birds and men, to name a few," Rybar states. "I knew that, after seeing them, one day I'd forge something similar.

Opposite page: *Starting from the top of Raymond Rybar Jr.'s incredible art knife are three ancient-Roman-type nails forged from carbon steel and formed into a handle and guard. Five rubies enliven the already spectacular handle, or hilt. The 21-inch blade is a composite of mosaics made up of nickel and high-carbon rods. The center is a bar of damascus that Rybar forged from tool steel, nickel, and Tama-Hagane and soft iron. There is also a jelly-roll pattern made up of the same material. Rybar placed the bars of mosaics, damascus and Tama-Hagane into high-carbon powder and forged them solid. Once completed, he fashioned a presentation stand from a mesquite stump with rare "Eucryptite" stones wedged into a split in the wood.* **(PointSeven photo)**

The 12 ½-inch blade of Raymond Rybar Jr.'s D-guard bowie is a multi-billet composite consisting of a high-carbon-steel-and-nickel-damascus bar of 11,000 layers making up the gray background. The bar was cut and sandwiched between 12 pieces of Tama Hagane and high-nickel and iron meteorite, the latter of which had been blended with enough wrought iron and nickel to get a solid consistency.

The grind of the blade is nearly flat with a convex edge. The D-guard is a much more common blend of 1095 blade steel and nickel with a forged-bird-head ripper that has been polished and blued. An ebony handle completes the piece. (PointSeven photo)

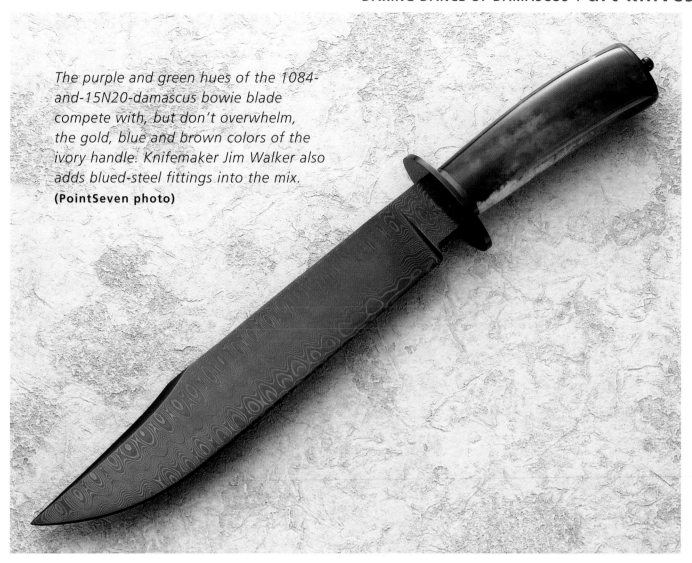

The purple and green hues of the 1084-and-15N20-damascus bowie blade compete with, but don't overwhelm, the gold, blue and brown colors of the ivory handle. Knifemaker Jim Walker also adds blued-steel fittings into the mix.
(PointSeven photo)

Jim Walker forged the ocean-plant-life-looking mosaic-damascus blade of his art bowie using 1084, 15N20 and O-1 blade steels. The bowie, which won the "Best Damascus Design" award at the 2004 Spirit of Steel Show, also sports an ivory handle and nickel-silver fittings.
(Hoffman photo)

ART OF THE KNIFE

Right: Thomas Haslinger achieved a great balance between form and function with his upscale hunter, something he accomplished by choosing the right materials and giving the knife subtle enhancements. The weave-pattern damascus blade is striking, especially when combined with the HCK Fingerprint damascus bolsters, walrus-ivory handle and file work. He fastened the bolsters to the knife tang with hidden pins so they don't interfere with the damascus patterns. Montana's own D. Reeves engraved the pinwheel patterns on the pin heads of the handle. **(SharpByCoop.com photo)**

Opposite page: Thomas Haslinger's two-finger bird & trout knife showcases a Chris Marks damascus blade and bolsters and an equally high-patterned stabilized curly koa wood handle. All the joints between the wood and metal have been ever so slightly rounded to prevent any sharp edges should the wood ever move. **(SharpByCoop.com photo)**

What isn't there to like about this knife? The way the grays of the acid-etched damascus blade match incredibly well with the wooly-mammoth-tooth handle is a good start. The fact that there is a wooly-mammoth-tooth handle is noteworthy in and of itself. The rubies set into the damascus bolsters are nice, subtle touches. The Americanized tanto blade is hot, the blue-anodized and jeweled liners are quite handsome, and the Spyderco hole in the blade makes for easy one-hand opening.
(PointSeven photo)

WES CRAWFORD grew up in the knifemaking shop of his dad, Pat, and as Wes grew older and needed money, there was always something that needed to be done. There were sheaths to be sewn and blades to cut. Wes did more and more until he was in the shop every day and doing just about everything there was to do in the knifemaking process. That's how Pat and Wes became a knifemaking team.

"I began making knives, in 1972, as a hobby, mostly to see if I could," Pat, an accountant at that time, recalls. "Back then there wasn't a whole lot of literature on the subject, so my first knives were the results of many trials and more errors, not to mention cuts and bruises. My staff of accountants started to wonder what I was doing when I showed up for work on Monday mornings with my hands covered in Band-Aids."

Francesco Pachi forged the dashing high-carbon-damascus blade of his hidden-tang art knife to celebrate a decade of knifemaking in 2001. He fashionably outfitted the piece with a premium-stag handle. (Pachi photo)

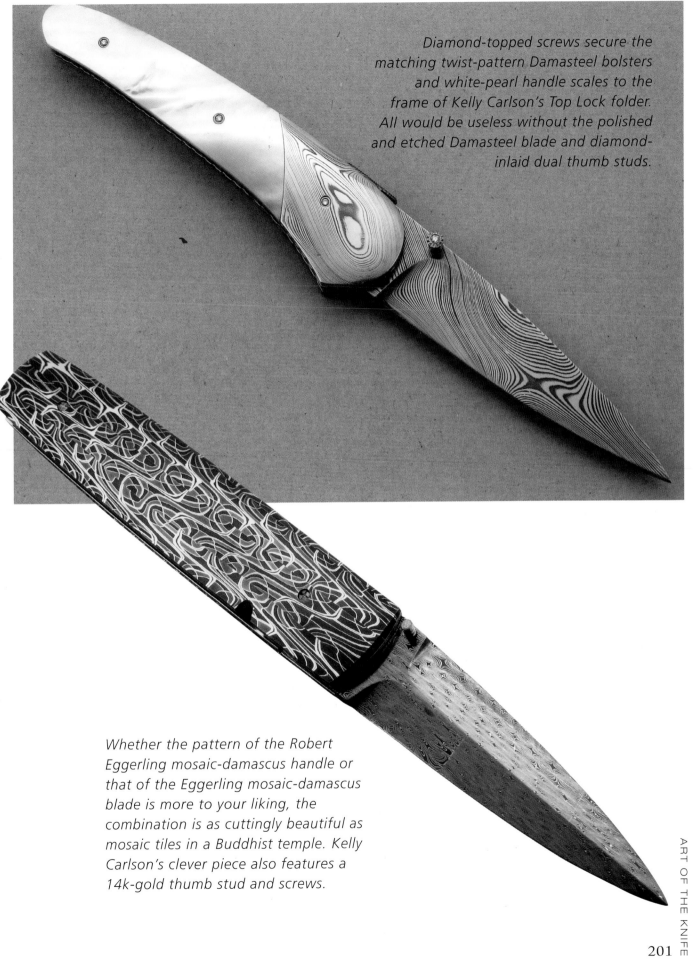

Diamond-topped screws secure the matching twist-pattern Damasteel bolsters and white-pearl handle scales to the frame of Kelly Carlson's Top Lock folder. All would be useless without the polished and etched Damasteel blade and diamond-inlaid dual thumb studs.

Whether the pattern of the Robert Eggerling mosaic-damascus handle or that of the Eggerling mosaic-damascus blade is more to your liking, the combination is as cuttingly beautiful as mosaic tiles in a Buddhist temple. Kelly Carlson's clever piece also features a 14k-gold thumb stud and screws.

Opposite page: *Large and small explosions reveal themselves in the blade and bolster steel of John Davis's gentleman's folding knife. John finished the blade and bolsters with a baking lacquer. He also niter-blued and file worked the liners, inlaid a topaz in the thumb stud and added a mastodon-ivory handle.* (**SharpByCoop.com** photo)

John Davis forged the blade of his chef's knife using a center core of 1084 high-carbon steel sandwiched between two complex, heat-blued and picturesque outer layers of mosaic damascus. Bottles, wine glasses, leaves and bunches of grapes are the subject matter of the wine-colored blade, all complemented by a stabilized-redwood handle with a Turkish walnut spacer. (**SharpByCoop.com** photo)

Anders Hogstrom and Conny Persson collaborated on "The Tucan," a knife named for its toucan-beak-shaped blade. The mosaic-damascus blade is forged to reveal images of toucans within the steel. An ancient-walrus-ivory handle, and textured and antiqued bronze fittings anchor the piece. (**Hogstrom** photo)

A fancy dresser, Francesco Pachi's folding knife
mixes plaid with polka dots seamlessly. It parades
a high-carbon-damascus blade and bolsters, and
a black-lip-pearl handle. Collector Pierluigi Peroni
shelled out the necessary dough for the fine folder.
(Francesco Pachi photo)

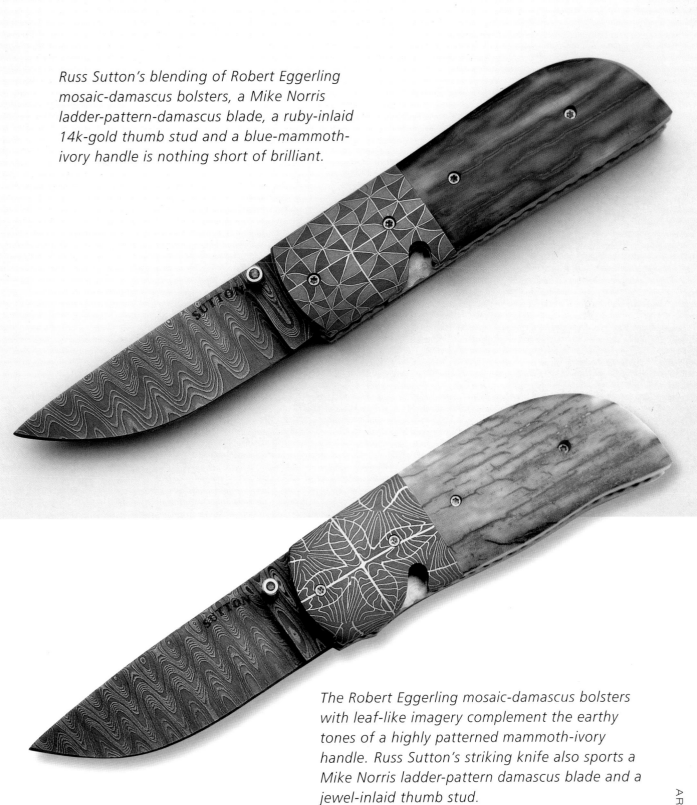

Russ Sutton's blending of Robert Eggerling mosaic-damascus bolsters, a Mike Norris ladder-pattern-damascus blade, a ruby-inlaid 14k-gold thumb stud and a blue-mammoth-ivory handle is nothing short of brilliant.

The Robert Eggerling mosaic-damascus bolsters with leaf-like imagery complement the earthy tones of a highly patterned mammoth-ivory handle. Russ Sutton's striking knife also sports a Mike Norris ladder-pattern damascus blade and a jewel-inlaid thumb stud.

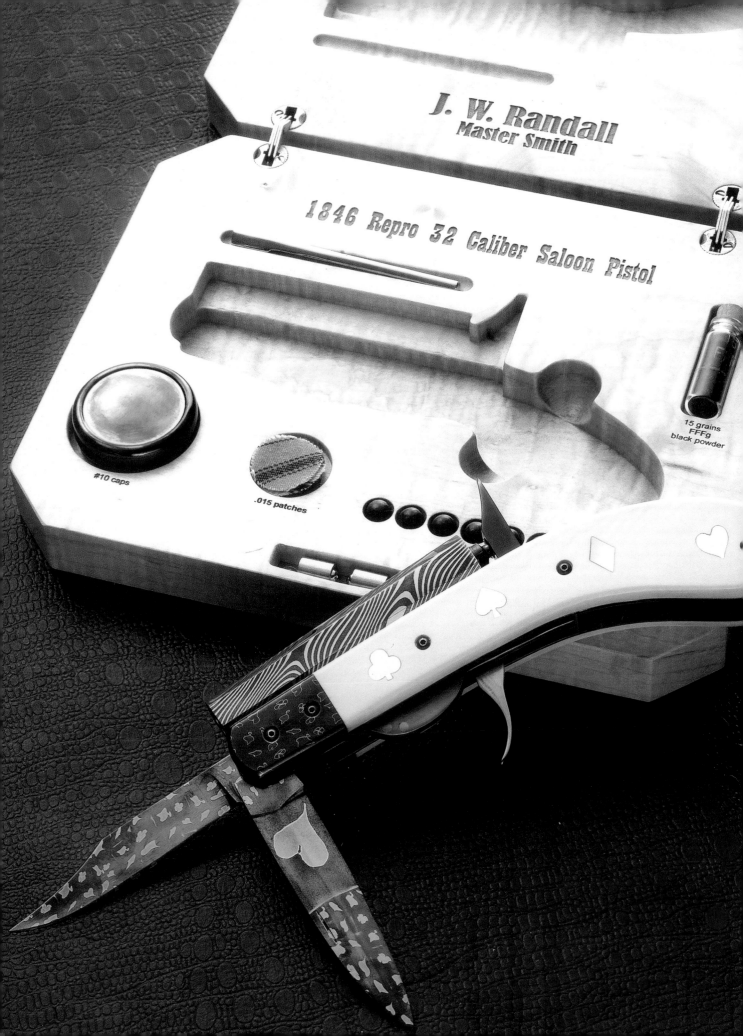

J.W. Randall's "Knight In Shining Armor Bowie" is aptly named for the basket-weave-pattern, mosaic-damascus blade forge welded to include images of a medieval knight. The piece also showcases nickel silver fittings and a water-buffalo-horn handle with knightly mother-of-pearl inlays. **(PointSeven photo)**

J.W. RANDALL is a master smith from Louisiana with rare talent and great dedication to his craft. Forging blades from damascus, he is an active member of the American Bladesmith Society and an advocate of the Bill Moran School of Bladesmithing.

"I make knives because of the creative release it gives me. I derive great personal satisfaction from providing a customer with a functional and artistic tool," Randall remarks. "I want my customers to view their purchases as sound investments and family heirlooms."

Opposite page: *An 1864 Unwin Rodgers saloon pistol/knife replica, J.W. Randall's latest mind-blowing piece features mosaic-damascus blades pattern-welded to include playing-card suits within the steel, gold-lip-pearl-inlaid ivory handle scales, a twist-damascus gun barrel, heat-colored bolsters and a heat-colored stainless steel frame. The pistol fires .32 caliber black powder percussions.* **(PointSeven photo)**

ART OF THE KNIFE

HUNTERS
CAN BE ART
KNIVES

A matched pair of Herman Schneider hunters is waiting to take its spot in a gun-and-knife collection. It would have to be a high-end collection, one with room for a couple of 154CM fixed blades featuring Sambar-stag handles and 303 stainless steel fittings. The twosome is hand finished to a high sheen. (Hiro Soga photo)

Hammered, or speckled, brass bolsters are the centerpieces of a Pete Truncali hunting knife that also features a dyed-bone handle, mosaic pins, a 3 5/8-inch ATS-34 blade and fancy file work along the blade spine and tang, as well as on the heads of the screws.
(PointSeven photo)

File work on all of PETE TRUNCALI'S knives is accomplished with a Dremel tool and files, according to the maker. "I don't particularly like plain guards and bolsters, and since I haven't learned engraving, I came up with the idea to speckle [hammer] the bolsters," he says. "I think it gives a knife a better look. All handles are screwed together, and I do file work on the heads of the screws." Truncali also fashions all sheaths by hand.

To be influenced by another artist to the point of wanting to emulate his or her very style and character, to reproduce and replicate models and patterns, this is the highest compliment one craftsman can pay to another. And to reciprocate the good gesture, to permit the replication to occur is to return the compliment. Such is the relationship between the apprentice and now master of his own renown, S.R. Johnson, and his one-time teacher, R.W. Loveless. Johnson fashioned a trio of Loveless-designed "Lambs," all with skinner blades. Note the unique "Loveless Design" tang stamps or trademarks, the ivory handles and other attention to details. (PointSeven photo)

Two of Germany's greatest knifemakers and artists—Jurgen Steinau and Dietmar Kressler—combined forces to bring together an integral inter-frame art knife with mosaic-pearl inlays. An expert tile layer couldn't have fit the pearl pieces together in a more inspiring way. It was the first collaborative effort between Steinau and Kressler. (Francesco Pachi photo)

No ordinary drop-point hunter, the fully integral "Lamb" from Ricardo Velarde started as one billet of steel before the maker cut, ground, sanded, buffed and honed it into a drop-point hunter. The handle is walrus ivory and the look is extraordinary.
(Francesco Pachi photo)

Thad Buchanan's stag-handle bird & trout knife features a mirror-polished, hollow-ground CPM 154CM blade with a full, tapered tang, a thin red liner and a 416 stainless steel guard. (Mitch Lum photo)

THAD BUCHANAN won an award for "Best New Maker" at his very first knife show in 1987. "After that, I was hooked," he says. "I spent as much time in the shop as I could and made a point of attending a show every few months. Unfortunately, life got busy in the early '90s and I put shows on the backburner. I continued to make knives for local customers and the slower pace allowed me to focus on improving the quality of my work."

A Thad Buchanan piece, the small knife is designed to cape big game. Such is accomplished using a 3 ¼-inch CPM 154CM blade, a giraffe-bone handle and stainless steel guard. (Mitch Lum photo)

The "Mountain Hunter" takes its handle from the woods, brass from the earth and its steel from the fires down below. Knifemaker Ralph Richards put it all together. (Ward photo)

"I forged a knife back in the 1960s with the help of two blacksmiths and I feel fortunate to have been able to work under their stern leadership," says RALPH RICHARDS. "Since then, my interests ran the gamut from woodcarving and tool making to knifemaking. I love woodcarving, but my passion is knifemaking."

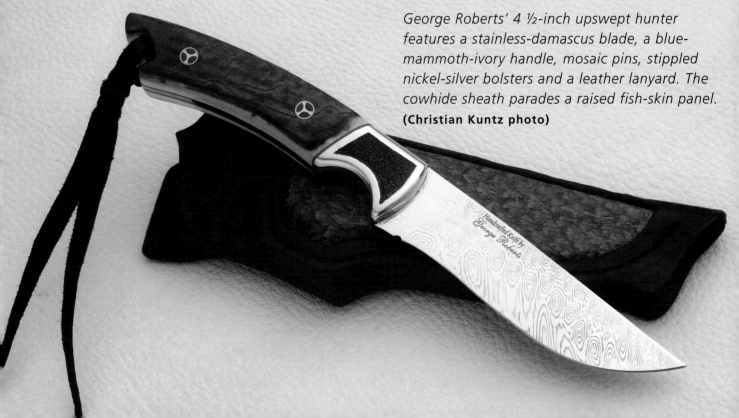

George Roberts' 4 ½-inch upswept hunter features a stainless-damascus blade, a blue-mammoth-ivory handle, mosaic pins, stippled nickel-silver bolsters and a leather lanyard. The cowhide sheath parades a raised fish-skin panel. (Christian Kuntz photo)

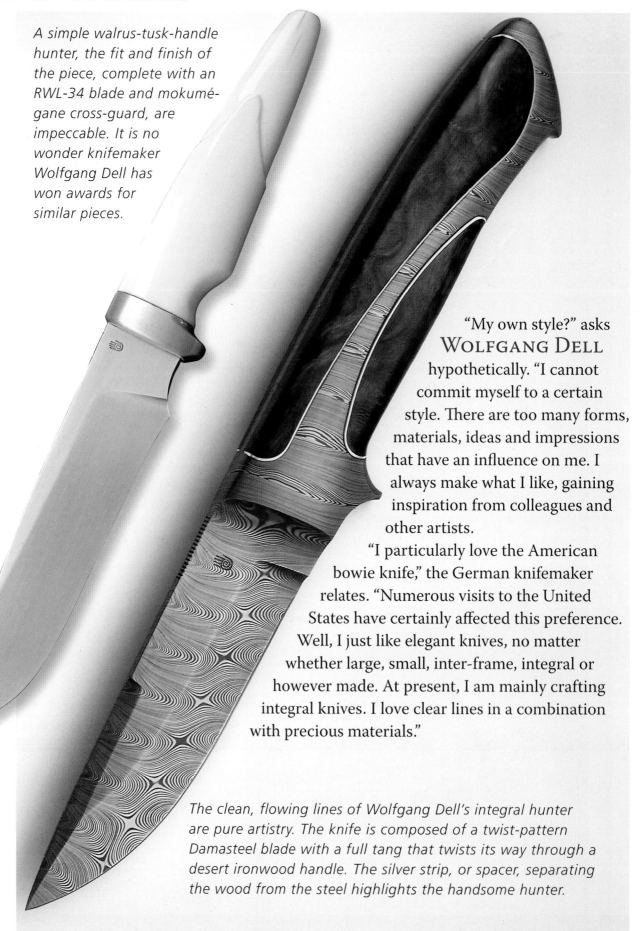

A simple walrus-tusk-handle hunter, the fit and finish of the piece, complete with an RWL-34 blade and mokumé-gane cross-guard, are impeccable. It is no wonder knifemaker Wolfgang Dell has won awards for similar pieces.

"My own style?" asks WOLFGANG DELL hypothetically. "I cannot commit myself to a certain style. There are too many forms, materials, ideas and impressions that have an influence on me. I always make what I like, gaining inspiration from colleagues and other artists.

"I particularly love the American bowie knife," the German knifemaker relates. "Numerous visits to the United States have certainly affected this preference. Well, I just like elegant knives, no matter whether large, small, inter-frame, integral or however made. At present, I am mainly crafting integral knives. I love clear lines in a combination with precious materials."

The clean, flowing lines of Wolfgang Dell's integral hunter are pure artistry. The knife is composed of a twist-pattern Damasteel blade with a full tang that twists its way through a desert ironwood handle. The silver strip, or spacer, separating the wood from the steel highlights the handsome hunter.

Wolfgang Dell's small semi-skinner parades an ironwood grip and a deep-cooled D-2 blade that reaches 60 Rc on the Rockwell Hardness scale.

"I have chosen the hand of the Hopi as my blade logo. This Indian ethnic sign symbolizes peace and the source of all life—water. It signalizes quietness and calmness for me, and a deep connection to nature," Wolfgang Dell explains. "My philosophy is quite simple: Every new knife should get a little better than the previous one. But as this is so, no one piece is perfect. I continuously try to improve my autodidactic skills in order to get closer to my vision of perfection."

Simplicity in design and embellishment reveals itself in the form of "Raindance," a Colten Tippetts partial-tang fixed blade. Among the amenities are a Devin Thomas raindrop-damascus blade, an Idaho elk antler handle with a buffalo-horn spacer, and a polished-nickel-silver guard.

Earthy tones highlight the George Roberts skinning knife, including the brown of the giraffe-bone handle, the chocolate color of the mokumé bolsters and the brass of the mosaic pins. The blade is file-worked Damasteel, and the sheath is hand-formed and hand-tooled cowhide. (Christian Kuntz photo)

Below: *In fashioning his version of a drop-point skinning knife, George Roberts of Yukon, Canada, combined a mammoth-ivory handle with a file-worked Damasteel blade. Perhaps maybe even more intriguing is the carved "inuksuk" on the stippled-nickel-silver bolsters. "Inuksuk" is an Inuit word meaning a stone monument. The Inuit, who were the first people to inhabit portions of Alaska, used such stone monuments for communication and survival. These stone figures were placed on the temporal and spiritual landscapes. Among many practical functions, they were employed as hunting and navigation aids, coordination points, indicators and message centers.* **(Christian Kuntz photo)**

Bob Patrick's hunters showcase D-2 blades, 416 stainless steel guards and aluminum pommels. From left are a drop-point hunter with a buffalo-horn handle, a trailing-point skinner featuring a Sambar-stag grip, and a Woodcraft-style piece sporting a bone handle. (PointSeven photo)

"Sometime in the early '60s, I traded all my 45 records for a lever-action switchblade," admits BOB PATRICK. "All I remember now is that the knife was marked "Rostfrei" and the handle scales were green plastic. I opened and closed that knife until I wore it out.

"In about 1964, I made my first knife in metal shop. I swiped an old Nicholson file, and when the teacher wasn't watching, I ground it into a blade on the pedestal grinder," Patrick confesses. "It took about a month to finish, and the handle was right around 10 layers of good electrician's tape."

A waterbuck-horn handle anchors J.W. Randall's 1095 high-carbon-steel hunting knife, which also showcases a 416 stainless steel guard and a mortised tang. (Tammy T. Randall photo)

Winner of the "Judges Award" at the 2004 Badger Knife Show, Michael Kanter's hunter exhibits a file-worked CPM S60V blade, dovetailed cable-damascus bolsters with mild steel pins, a titanium spacer and an elephant ivory handle. It slips silently into a hand-stitched, vegetable-tanned sheath that features an elephant-hide overlay. **(PointSeven photo)**

It's the stabilized sheep-horn handle of Michael Kanter's hunter that gives it that groovy feel. Dovetailed mokumé bolsters are a nice touch, as are titanium, copper and brass spacers. The CPM S60V blade stretches 4 inches overall, and the knife comes with a hand-stitched, vegetable-tanned sheath featuring a crocodile-skin overlay. **(PointSeven photo)**

Above: The colors of the stabilized-mammoth-tooth spacer set off Michael Kanter's hunter. The knife also sports a walrus-ivory handle, a polished and file-worked BG-42 blade, and blue-anodized-titanium and brick-red-fiber spacers. Mosaic handle pins complete the piece.

(SharpByCoop.com photo)

The Thomas Gerner hunter/utility knife features a forged 5160 blade, a red-deer-antler handle, an Australian red ebony spacer and nickel silver fittings. (Pete Solvander photo, New Design Ltd.)

Two absolutely rare and collectible knives, Bob Loveless's drop-point hunter and semi-skinner are hidden-tang fixed blades dressed in stacked-leather handles. (Francesco Pachi photo)

R.W. LOVELESS maker Riverside, Calif.

R.W. LOVELESS maker Riverside, Calif.

CLASSICALLY STYLED STEEL

The inspiration for the Silver Mounted Dogbone Bowie is an early American-made dog-bone bowie knife with a Spanish notch—a curly ornamentation on the blade near the hilt—owned by L. Kimball of Vicksburg, Miss. The original bowie fetched $80,000 at a 1993 Butterfield and Butterfield auction in San Francisco.

As recorded on July 1, 1829, in the courthouse in Vicksburg, William Pescod paid a yearly salary of $1,000 to Loring Kimball for being a clerk in a mercantile business. At that time, Kimball sold his rights as a partner and equity in the firm of Pescod and Kimball to Pescod. The original knife was made for Kimball between 1829 and 1839 during the early days of the bowie knife. The bowie knife was in the American vocabulary before Col. James' death at the Alamo in March of 1836.

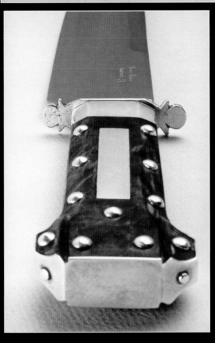

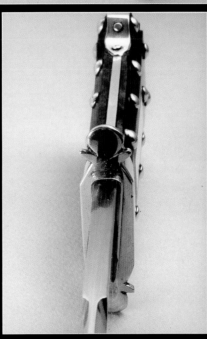

Batson's version of the knife features a forged high-carbon steel blade, 10 ½ inches long, a dense burly walnut handle, a German silver frame, 22 domed sterling silver handle pins, and sterling silver escutcheon plates, pommel wrap, ferrule and guard. (Buddy Thomason photos)

Collectors of edged art hold the name **JAMES BATSON** in high regard, he being one in the same who served as president of the American Bladesmith Society (ABS) from 1999 to 2003; an ABS master smith; an inductee into the ABS Hall of Fame; and the namesake behind the Alabama Forge Council's Batson Bladesmithing Symposium held for the past 18 years at Tannehill State Park near Bessemer, Ala.

Long before Batson forged his first blade in 1974, an American hero, Col. James Bowie, carried a knife that would change the way bladed objects were made forever. Batson has studied and extensively researched the life of Bowie, and the design and making of early American bowie knives. He has authored several magazine articles and hosted many James Bowie symposiums. In 1988, he wrote and published the book *James Bowie and the Sandbar Fight*. Batson is a life member of the Antique Bowie Knife Collectors Association and is known for his knowledge of early bowie knives.

The 7-inch, mosaic-damascus blade of the Horse Head Bowie consists of various damascus billets forged during Jim Batson's knifemaking career. The blue colors in the blade are the result of a 500-degree tempering temperature, and the mosaic damascus is a panel of various designs and metals surrounded by an 80-layer, aggressive, twisted-steel edge. The mosaic pattern that extends from the ricasso to the middle of the blade consists of eight horses' heads. The first horse head was forged from a 3-inch-square tube of powdered metal and a cookie cutter fashioned of pure nickel in the shape of the horse's head. The pommel and guard of the bowie are slices off the damascus billet, and the handle is the inside of a walrus tusk, a substance referred to as tapioca. **(Steven Michael Studios photo)**

The water-buffalo-horn handle is shaped and smoothed as if exposed to a century's worth of ocean waves. The ATS-34 blade is equally flawless and spotless, and accepts a stingray-skin-covered wood sheath with a buffalo-horn tip and throat.
(Hasegawa photo)

Japan's **YASUTAKA WADA** chooses natural handle materials for their marvelous quality. He files his knives by hand and rarely makes full-tang knives, explaining that narrow-tang pieces represent his art. With each knife purchased from him, Wada includes specifications written on chamois skin.

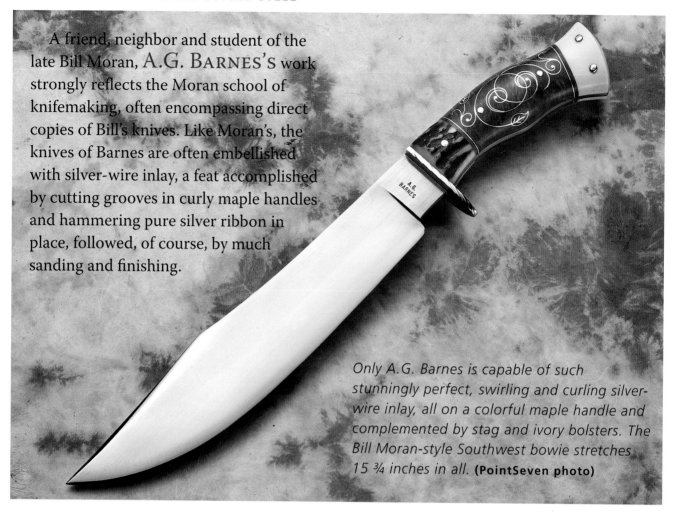

A friend, neighbor and student of the late Bill Moran, A.G. BARNES'S work strongly reflects the Moran school of knifemaking, often encompassing direct copies of Bill's knives. Like Moran's, the knives of Barnes are often embellished with silver-wire inlay, a feat accomplished by cutting grooves in curly maple handles and hammering pure silver ribbon in place, followed, of course, by much sanding and finishing.

Only A.G. Barnes is capable of such stunningly perfect, swirling and curling silver-wire inlay, all on a colorful maple handle and complemented by stag and ivory bolsters. The Bill Moran-style Southwest bowie stretches 15 ¾ inches in all. **(PointSeven photo)**

As a campfire warms one side of the curly maple handle, a wolf howls at the moon across the horizon. The 17 ½-inch camp knife comes from the hands of A.G. Barnes, a master smith who forged the 5160 blade.

(PointSeven photo)

Above: *The sexy and traditional Khanjar knife design is handled with panache by Bud Nealy, who built it using an ATS-34 blade, an ebony handle, Mike Sakmar mokumé bolsters and mosaic pins.*

Below: *The sensuous curves of silver wire accentuate an already curvaceous curly maple handle. A.G. Barnes built the piece as a replica of Bill Moran's ST-24 Fighter, and it comes with a cowhide-leather sheath.* **(PointSeven photo)**

Herman Schneider has been at the knife game a long time and is one of the most respected knifemakers in the world, not only for his skills, but also for the personalities of himself and his knives, the perfection of a craft and the building of honest collectors' items. Herman's Cross-guard Fighter showcases a hand-finished, double-vacuum-melted 154CM blade, a stag handle, nickel-silver handle wrap and 303 stainless steel fittings.

(Hiro Soga photo)

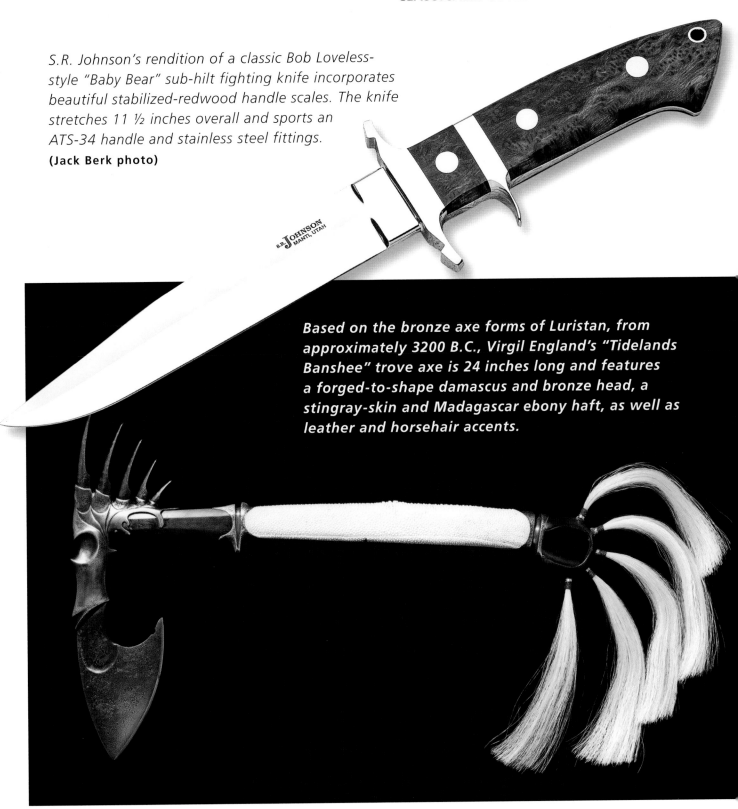

S.R. Johnson's rendition of a classic Bob Loveless-style "Baby Bear" sub-hilt fighting knife incorporates beautiful stabilized-redwood handle scales. The knife stretches 11 ½ inches overall and sports an ATS-34 handle and stainless steel fittings.

(Jack Berk photo)

Based on the bronze axe forms of Luristan, from approximately 3200 B.C., Virgil England's "Tidelands Banshee" trove axe is 24 inches long and features a forged-to-shape damascus and bronze head, a stingray-skin and Madagascar ebony haft, as well as leather and horsehair accents.

VIRGIL ENGLAND has been designing and making knives for 36 years. During the early 1970s, he made field knives, and then began working on weapons forms that have remained the focus of his work ever since. This has resulted in the creation of helmets, armor, pole arms, axes, swords and other weaponry. Everything he makes is done using the techniques of 10th-to-15th-century armorers.

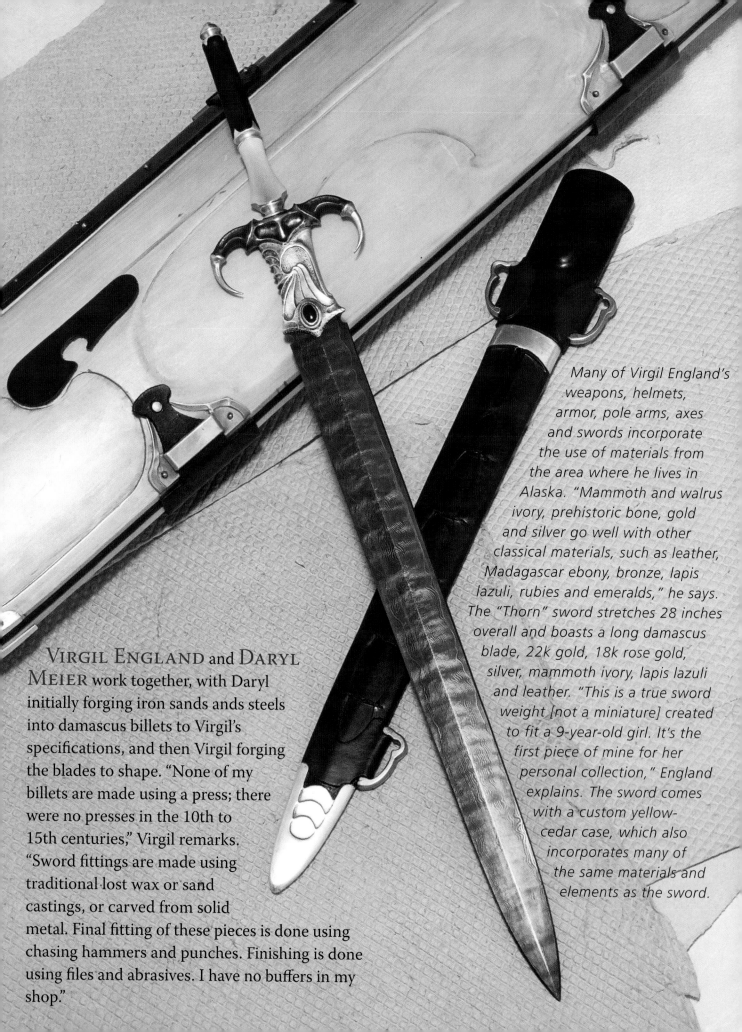

VIRGIL ENGLAND and DARYL MEIER work together, with Daryl initially forging iron sands ands steels into damascus billets to Virgil's specifications, and then Virgil forging the blades to shape. "None of my billets are made using a press; there were no presses in the 10th to 15th centuries," Virgil remarks. "Sword fittings are made using traditional lost wax or sand castings, or carved from solid metal. Final fitting of these pieces is done using chasing hammers and punches. Finishing is done using files and abrasives. I have no buffers in my shop."

Many of Virgil England's weapons, helmets, armor, pole arms, axes and swords incorporate the use of materials from the area where he lives in Alaska. "Mammoth and walrus ivory, prehistoric bone, gold and silver go well with other classical materials, such as leather, Madagascar ebony, bronze, lapis lazuli, rubies and emeralds," he says. The "Thorn" sword stretches 28 inches overall and boasts a long damascus blade, 22k gold, 18k rose gold, silver, mammoth ivory, lapis lazuli and leather. "This is a true sword weight [not a miniature] created to fit a 9-year-old girl. It's the first piece of mine for her personal collection," England explains. The sword comes with a custom yellow-cedar case, which also incorporates many of the same materials and elements as the sword.

A number of Michigan knifemakers build knives in the style of the late William Scagel, and Ron Welling is no exception. Ron is a quality knifemaker, as evidenced by the handsome duo folder/fixed blade with O-1 blades, a mammoth-bark-ivory handle, a silver arrow as a handle shield and a bronze guard. **(PointSeven photo)**

Though it is in the style of the late William Scagel, Ron Welling's dagger sports an unusual and modern blued, fire-pattern-damascus blade, a sculpted-bronze guard, leather, nickel-silver and ivory spacers, and a crown-stag handle butt. The sheath is nothing to sneeze at, either.
(PointSeven photo)

Both Scagel-style camp knives feature hand-forged 1084 steel blades, stacked-leather handles, brass guards and crown-stag end caps. Dr. Jim Lucie completed one of the knives in 2004 and one in 2006, and they differ by one inch in blade length and overall size. **(PointSeven photos)**

Dr. Jim Lucie was the personal physician of the late, great knifemaker WILLIAM SCAGEL. All of the spacers and some of the other fittings used in Lucie's Scagel-style knives were obtained from the late maker's workshop after his passing.

"My blade finish is accomplished by the use of stones, involving eight progressively finer grit stones, and then rubbed by hand with rottenstone paste," Lucie relates. "I use no buffing wheels whatsoever on any of my blades.

"An important aspect of the cutting edge of a Scagel-style knife is that no ground edge should be visible and the blade is ground to be convex, or 'apple seed,' in contour," he adds. "I use a Norton Multi-Stone rig to create the proper edge geometry, followed by 'steeling' with an extremely fine steel until all evidence of the wire edge is gone. When done properly, the result is an extremely sharp cutting edge with no visible ground line showing."

In closing, Lucie notes, "The leather spacers are stained with eight to 10 coats of a good, quality mahogany-colored dye, and the last step is to give the entire knife a well-rubbed coat of Butcher's Wax, which I happen to believe is the finest wax available."

The San Francisco bowie is one of the world's most recognizable style of knives, but none make them better than Jim Sornberger, who fashioned a piece with a 14k-gold handle wrap, handle inlays of red cinnabar and black-and-white gold quartz, and a 14k-gold and coin-silver sheath. A California quail is masterfully engraved on the finely handcrafted sheath. **(Michael Fong photo)**

Bud Nealy's collaborations with various martial artists have yielded the PTK (Pick Tactical Knife) deployed by the U.S. Army Special Forces Group 10, the Wortac (a collaboration with Kelly Worden), the Amoeba (Ralph Mroz) and the JKD (Jeet Kune Do, Joe Maffei). Bud's own Pesh-Kabz knife has gained notoriety over the years for its applications as a small, concealable fixed blade, its unusual grind and blade tip, and for the MCS II Sheath System with which it is sometimes married. This version of the Pesh-Kabz features finger grooves and a pointed pommel.

Edmund Davidson's style has its roots in the R.W. Loveless school of shape and design. "I have never made a true Loveless copy, but I have made integral knives using the Loveless shape and outline. Bob's shapes are pure genius, and I believe he has been gracious and generous in sharing his patterns," Davidson says. The knife pictured is Davidson's 100th Loveless design—a "lengthened straight hunter" of integral construction. It sports a BG-42 blade and integral bolsters engraved by Jere Davidson using a hammer and chisel. The handle scales are stabilized box elder. **(PointSeven photo)**

Graziano Cabona's first symmetrical dagger does not disappoint. Of hidden-tang construction, the knife features a premium stag handle and a polished look and feel.
(Francesco Pachi photo)

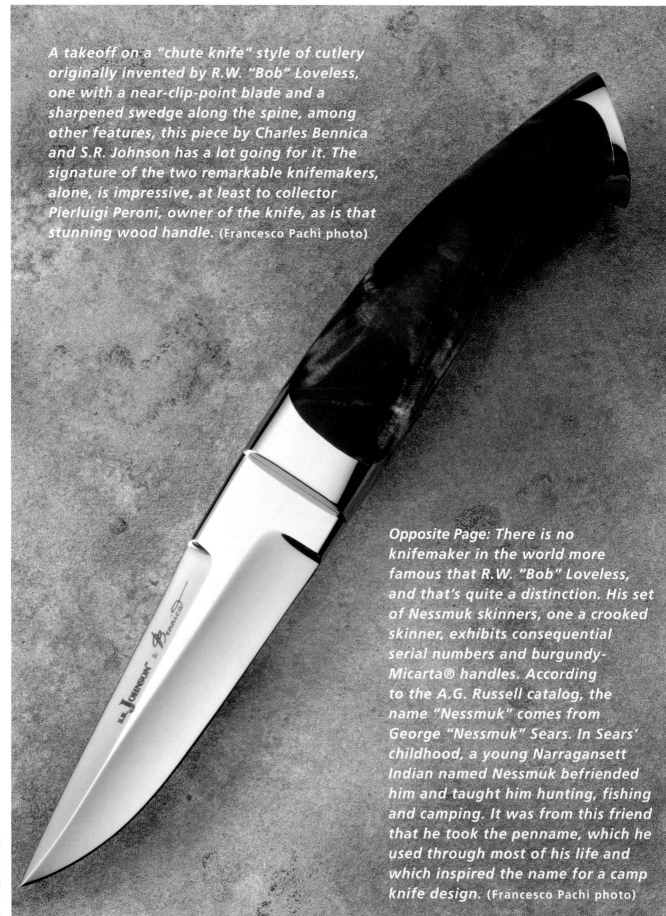

A takeoff on a "chute knife" style of cutlery originally invented by R.W. "Bob" Loveless, one with a near-clip-point blade and a sharpened swedge along the spine, among other features, this piece by Charles Bennica and S.R. Johnson has a lot going for it. The signature of the two remarkable knifemakers, alone, is impressive, at least to collector Pierluigi Peroni, owner of the knife, as is that stunning wood handle. (Francesco Pachi photo)

Opposite Page: There is no knifemaker in the world more famous that R.W. "Bob" Loveless, and that's quite a distinction. His set of Nessmuk skinners, one a crooked skinner, exhibits consequential serial numbers and burgundy-Micarta® handles. According to the A.G. Russell catalog, the name "Nessmuk" comes from George "Nessmuk" Sears. In Sears' childhood, a young Narragansett Indian named Nessmuk befriended him and taught him hunting, fishing and camping. It was from this friend that he took the penname, which he used through most of his life and which inspired the name for a camp knife design. (Francesco Pachi photo)

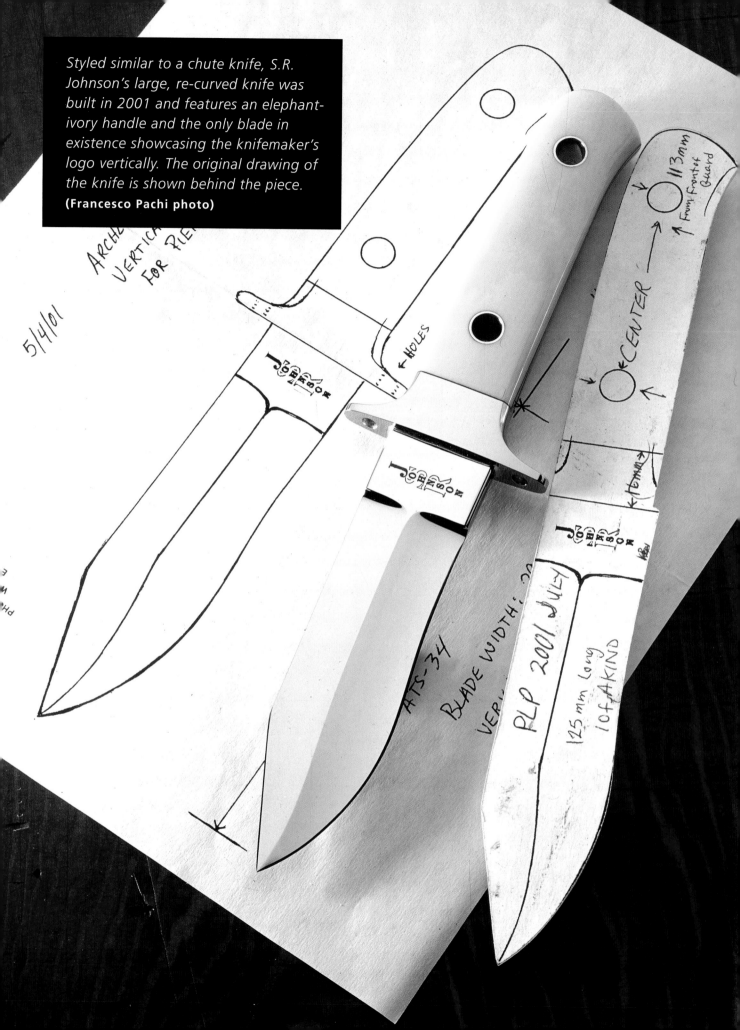

Styled similar to a chute knife, S.R. Johnson's large, re-curved knife was built in 2001 and features an elephant-ivory handle and the only blade in existence showcasing the knifemaker's logo vertically. The original drawing of the knife is shown behind the piece.
(Francesco Pachi photo)

A similar knife to Dan Dennehy's Alamo Bowie that is on display in the museum gift shop at the Alamo in San Antonio, Texas, this Dennehy piece sports a fully etched, hollow-ground, 12-inch blade. The words "Remember the Alamo! Remember Goliad! Thirteen Days of Glory Feb 23, 1836 Mar 6, 1836" are etched on one side of the blade, and the other side displays an eight-line poem that commemorates Travis' call for "defenders to step forward." The handle is elephant ivory inlayed with 18 turquoise cabochons.

(Custom Knife Gallery of Colorado photo)

A Scandinavian-style "Tolleknive" art knife, Tom Bache-Wiig's piece dons a sperm-whale-tooth and acrylic-stabilized-birch-burl handle, a sterling-silver bolster and an Uddeholm Elmax powdered-stainless-steel blade.

ART OF THE KNIFE

241

Michael McClure's reproduction of a Joseph Rogers bowie incorporates a 6-inch, flat-ground 5160 blade with a false edge along the spine, a nickel-silver, pinned and soldered double guard, and a Sambar-stag handle. The traditionally styled sheath is blind-stitched leather with a nickel-silver throat and tip.
(PointSeven photo)

Working in the family glass business in Western Pennsylvania, MICHAEL MCCLURE had the opportunity to learn a little about beveling glass for mirrors. "Too tedious for a youngster, I moved on to glazing, working for the past 30 years in the San Francisco Bay area," McClure explains.

"Taking an early retirement, I realized I needed something to occupy my time. Having always been interested in knives, even to the point of making some since the 1980s, it was natural for me to pursue that endeavor. As an American Bladesmith Society journeyman smith, the majority of my work involves the hand-forged blade."

In the style of the known knifemaker Bob Loveless, Dietmar Kressler's "Big Bear" sub-hilt fighter incorporates an impressive desert-ironwood handle attached to the full tang with six pins on each side. (Francesco Pachi photo)

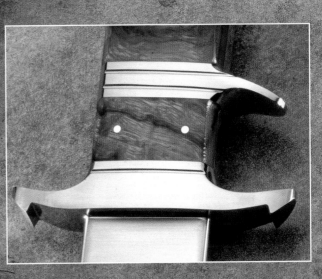

Scott Slobodian's "Sword of Doom" showcases a 29-inch 1050 high-carbon-steel blade that has been clay tempered, ground and finished by hand, a silk-wrapped, stingray-skin handle, a stone-vine-wood saya (scabbard), and fittings of sterling silver, iron, Merlin gold, amber and buffalo horn.

With obvious Japanese influence, or rather, in the Japanese style, is Scott Slobodian's "Red Dragon" tanto featuring a clay-tempered 1050 blade with distinct hamon (temper line), *a traditional silk-wrapped stingray-skin handle, Merlin-gold menuki (handle charms), and a buffalo-horn and carved-gold spacer.* (Slobodian photo)

A SMATTERING OF
SLIP JOINTS
SAVED FOR
LAST

Dan Burke's half whittler is gussied up in a black-lip-pearl handle with inlays shaped like calla lilies. Dan formed the flowers from sea-snail shell, pink pearl and abalone, while the flower stems are sterling silver. The blades, which seem secondary in this case, are BG-42.
(PointSeven photo)

"What I make are mainly gentlemen's and exhibition knives in patterns that date back anywhere from 1800-1920," says DAN BURKE. "I try to design similar knives to the exhibition pieces from Sheffield, England. During the late-19th and early-20th centuries, complex and delicate pocketknife patterns were the norm. I do my best to duplicate such styles using exotic handle materials like exhibition-grade pearl, tortoise shell and ivory."

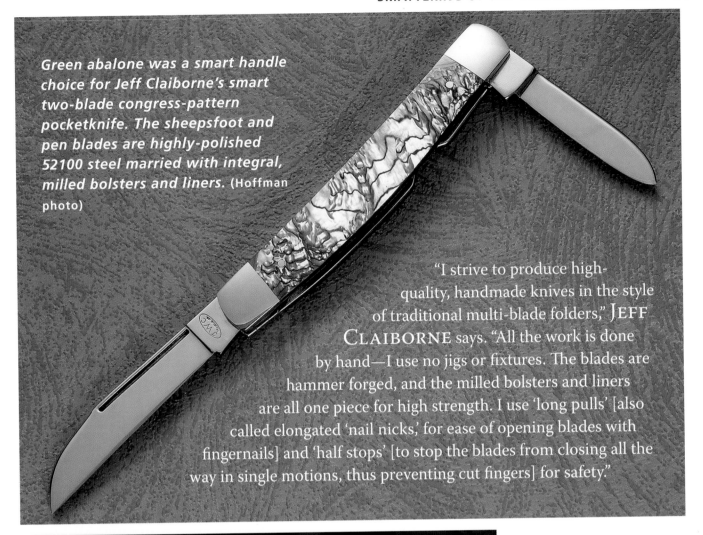

Green abalone was a smart handle choice for Jeff Claiborne's smart two-blade congress-pattern pocketknife. The sheepsfoot and pen blades are highly-polished 52100 steel married with integral, milled bolsters and liners. (Hoffman photo)

"I strive to produce high-quality, handmade knives in the style of traditional multi-blade folders," JEFF CLAIBORNE says. "All the work is done by hand—I use no jigs or fixtures. The blades are hammer forged, and the milled bolsters and liners are all one piece for high strength. I use 'long pulls' [also called elongated 'nail nicks,' for ease of opening blades with fingernails] and 'half stops' [to stop the blades from closing all the way in single motions, thus preventing cut fingers] for safety."

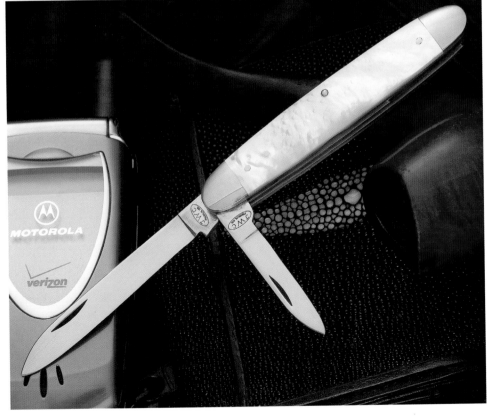

Spear and pen blades of 52100 steel butt up against nickel-silver bolsters and liners, and a white-mother-of-pearl handle. Knifemaker Jeff Claiborne refers to the crescent-shaped nail nicks as "eyelash pulls." **(Hoffman photo)**

ART OF THE KNIFE

247

Fifty rubies set in 14k gold grace the mother-of-pearl handle of Dan Burke's English gentleman's jackknife. The pocket folder measures 3 1/8 inches closed and sports BG-42 blades, a coin-edged spacer, and stainless steel bolsters and liners. (PointSeven photo)

Dan Burke's fly-fishing knife features a sheepsfoot main blade, a hook dislodging/fish scaling blade and a third implement that acts as a "vice" for holding hooks while tying flies. Other accessories include a fly-fishing pick and tweezers, and a checkered mastodon-ivory handle, complete with a carving of a trout. (PointSeven photo)

French piqué work on the antique-tortoise-shell handle is only the start of a Dan Burke wharncliffe whittler. Simon Lytton engraved the bolsters and spacers to further enliven the three-blade pocketknife. **(PointSeven photo)**

C. Gray Taylor says the "orange blossom"-pattern pocketknife was the most expensive style of folder to make at the time it was initially manufactured. Taylor's rendition features ATS-34 blades, including a manicure implement, 416 stainless steel liners and bolsters, a presentation-grade black-lip-pearl handle and 14k-gold raised pins and shield. (PointSeven photo)

C. GRAY TAYLOR made his first multi-blade folding knife in the early 1980s and says it was an honor to sell it to fellow knifemaker Steve Hoel. "Since then I have made mostly traditional multi-blade lobster patterns and period pieces. I do all my own work, which includes profiling the knife and blade, carving, inlay work, and heat-treating the blades and springs. The only exception to this is engraving," Taylor notes. "Heat-treating is such an important part of the process, especially on the multi-blade folders where I always check the hardness of each blade and spring."

ART OF THE KNIFE

251

C. Gray Taylor fashioned a "sleeve-board lobster pattern" slip joint with scissors. Materials include ATS-34 blade and implement steel, 14k gold and antique tortoise shell. The maker inlaid the shell handle with pink, green, white and yellow gold grapes and vines. Tim George accomplished the shading on the leaves. **(PointSeven photo)**

CONTACT THESE ART OF THE KNIFE MAKERS

Stefan Albert, Lucenecka 434/4, 986 01 Filakovo, Slovak Republik; phone: +421.908.966.261, Stefan.albert@post.sk, www.albertknives.com

Jens Anso, GL. Skanderborgvej 116, 8472 sporup, Denmark; phone: +45.8696.8826, www.ansoknives.com, info@ansoknives.com.

George Baartman, POB 1116, Warmbaths, Limpopo Province, South Africa 0480; phone: +27.14.736.4036, thabathipa@gmail.com

Tom Bache-Wiig, Haugane, 5966 Eivindvik, Norway; www.tombachewiig.com, tom.bache-wiig@enivest.net

A.G. Barnes, 11341 Rock Hill Rd., Hagerstown, MD 21740-1957; phone: 301.223.4587, a.barnes@myactv.net

Lee Gene Baskett, 427 Sutzer Creek Rd., Eastview, KY 42732; phone: 270.862.5019, baskettknives@hotmail.com, www.geocities.com/baskettknives

James Batson, 311 Fox Ridge Rd., Douglas, GA 31535; phone: 256.971.6860

Gaetan Beauchamp, 125, de la Riviere, Stoneham, QC, Canada G0A 4P0; phone: 418.848.1914, knives@gbeauchamp.ca, www.gbeauchamp.ca

Charles Bennica, Chemin du Salet, 34190 Moules et Baucels, France; phone: +33.4.67.73.42.40, b-ni-k@club-internet.fr

Jim Blair (engraver), POB 64, Glenrock, WY 82637; phone: 307.436.8115

Robert Blasingame, 281 Swanson, Kilgore, TX 75662; phone: 903.984.8144

Arpad Bojtos, Dobsinseho 10, 98403 Lucenec, Slovakia; phone: 011.421.4743.33512, bojtos@stonline.sk, www.arpadbojtos.sk

Philip Booth, 301 S. Jeffery Ave., Ithaca, MI 48847; phone: 989.875.2844

Sandra Brady (scrimshaw artist), POB 104, Monclova, OH 43542; phone: 419.866.0435, www.scrimshawbysandrabrady.com

Ed Brandsey, 335 Forest Lake Dr., Milton, WI 53563; phone: 608.868.9010

David Brodziak, P.O. Box 1130, Albany, Western Australia 6331; phone: (08) 9841.3314, www.brodziakcustomknives.com, brodziak@omninet.net.au

Thad Buchanan, 915 N.W. Perennial Way, Prineville, OR 97754; phone: 541.416.2556

Dan Burke, 22001 Ole Barn Rd., Edmond, OK 73013; phone: 405.341.3406

Graziano Cabona, Via Roma, 40, 25063-Gardone V.T. (BS) Italy

Kelly Carlson, 54 S. Holt Hill, Antrim, NH 03440; phone: 603.588.2765, kellycarlson@tds.net, www.carlsonknives.com

Fred Carter, 5219 Deer Creek Rd., Wichita Falls, TX 76302; phone: 904.723.4020

Jeff Claiborne, 1470 Roberts Rd., Franklin, IN 46131; phone: 317.736.7443

Bill Coffey, 68 Joshua, Clovis, CA 93611

Lamont Coombs Jr., 546 State Rt. 46, Bucksport, ME 04416; phone: 207.469.3057, theknifemaker@hotmail.com

Pat and Wes Crawford, 205 N. Center, W. Memphis, AR 72301; phone: 870.732.2452, www.crawfordknives.com

Edmund Davidson, 3345 Virginia Ave., Goshen, VA 24439; phone: 540.997.5651, www.edmunddavidson.com

John Davis, 235 Lampe Rd., Selah, WA 98942; 509.697.3845

Wolfgang Dell, Am Alten Berg 9, 73277 Owen-Teck, Germany; phone: +49.0.7021.81802, Wolfgang@dell-knives.de, www.dell-knives.de

Dan Dennehy, POB 2F, Del Norte, CO 81132; phone: 719.657.2545

Johannes Ebner, Pingitzzerkai 2, A-5400 Hallein/Salzburg, Austria; phone: 0043(0)6245/804.54, www.johannesebner.com

Virgil England, 1340 Birchwood St., Anchorage, AK 99508; phone: 907.274.9494, www.virgilengland.com, hardfistdown@acsalaska.net

Vince Evans, 35 Beaver Creek Rd., Cathlamet, WA 98612; phone: 360.795.0096, vevans@localnet.com, www.arscives.com/vevans

Dick Faust, 624 Kings Hwy. N, Rochester, NY 14617; phone: 585.544.1948

Tom Ferry, 16005 S.E. 322 St., Auburn, WA 98092; phone: 253.939.4468, Knfesmth71@aol.com, www.tferryknives.com

Dennis Friedly, 12 Cottontail Ln. E, Cody, WY 82414; phone: 307.527.6811, friedly_knives@hotmail.com

Frank Gamble, 4676 Commercial St. SE, #26, Salem, OR 97302; phone: 503.581.7993

Thomas Gerner, P.O. Box 301, Walpole 6398, Western Australia; gerner@westnet.com.au

Pedro Gibert, Gutierrez 5189 Rama Caida, 5603 San Rafael, Mendoza, Argentina; phone: 054.2627.441138, rosademayo@infovia.com.ar, pedrogibert@hotmail.com

David Goldberg, 1120 Blyth Ct., Blue Bell, PA 19422; phone: 215.654.7117

Ernie Grospitch, 18440 Amityville Dr., Orlando, FL 32820; phone: 407.568.5438, www.erniesknives.com

Don Hanson III, POB 13, Success, MO 65570; phone: 573.674.3045, www.sunfishforge.com, www.donhansonknives.com

Jim Harrison, 721 Fairington View Dr., St. Louis, MO 63129; phone: 314.894.2525, www.seamusknives.com

Kevin and Heather Harvey, POB 768, Belfast 1100, South Africa; phone: 27.13.253.0914, heavin.knives@mweb.co.za, www.africut.co.za

Thomas Haslinger, 164 Fairview Dr. SE, Calgary, Alberta, Canada T2H 1B3; phone: 403.253.9628, Thomas@haslinger-knives.com

Wally Hayes, 1026 Old Montreal Rd., Orleans, Ontario, Canada K4A 3N2; phone: 613.824.9520, www.hayesknives.com, hayesknives@hayesknives.com

Richard Hehn, Lehnmuehler Str. 1, 55444 Dorrebach, Germany; phone: 06724.3152

E. Jay Hendrickson, 4204 Ballenger Creek Pike, Frederick, MD 21703; phone: 301.663.6923, jhendrickson@xecu.net

Wayne Hensley, 2924 Glad Date Dr., Conyers, GA 30094; phone: 770.483.8938

Tim Herman, 7721 Foster, Overland Park, KS 66204; phone: 913.649.3860

Bill and Nancy Herndon, 32520 Michigan St., Acton, CA 93510; phone: 661.269.5860, bherndons1@earthlink.net

Don Hethcoat, Box 1764, Clovis, NM 88102; phone: 505.762.5721, dhethcoat@plateautel.net

Gil Hibben, POB 13, LaGrange, KY 40031; phone: 502.222.1397

Harumi Hirayama, 4-5-13, Kitamachi, Warabi-City, Saitama.335-0001 Japan; phone/fax: 81.48.443.2248, www.ne.jp/asahi/harumi/knives

Howard Hitchmough, 95 Old Street Rd., Peterborough, NH 03458; phone: 603.924.9646, howard@hitchmoughknives.com

Kevin Hoffman, 28 Hopeland Dr., Savannah, GA 31419; phone: 912.920.3579, www.KLHoffman.com

Ralph Hoffmann and Sabine Piper, Forsterweg 108 a, 22525 Hamburg, Germany; phone: +49.0.40.5402419, Hoffmann-piper@web.de

Anders Hogstrom, Granvagen 2, 135 52 Tyreso, Sweden; phone: +46.8.798.5802, www.andershogstrom.com, andershogstrom@rixmail.se

Rob Hudson, 340 Roush Rd., Northumberland, PA 17857; phone: 570.473.9588, robscustknives@aol.com

John Lewis Jensen, 530 S. Madison Ave. #14, Pasadena, CA 91101; phone: 323.559.7454, john@jensenknives.com

Steven R. Johnson, 202 E. 200 N, Manti, UT 84642; phone: 435.835.7941, www.srjknives.com, srj@mail.manti.com

Michael Kanter, 14550 W. Honey Ln., New Berlin, WI 53151; phone: 262.860.1136, mike@adammichaelknives.com, www.adammichaelknives.com

Linda Karst-Stone (scrimshaw artist), 903 Tanglewood Ln., Kerrville, TX 78028; phone: 830.896.4678, karstone@ktc.com

Jot Singh Khalsa, 368 Village St., Millis, MA 02054; phone: 508.376.8162, www.khalsakirpans.com

Shiva Ki, 5222 Ritterman Ave., Baton Rouge, LA 70805; phone: 225.356.7274, www.shivakicustomknives.com

Joe Kious, 1015 Ridge Pointe Rd., Kerrville, TX 78028; phone: 830.367.2277, kious@ktc.com

Terry Knipschield, 808 12th Ave. NE, Rochester, MN 55906; phone: 507.288.7829, knipper01@charter.net

Steven Koster, 16261 Gentry Ln., Huntington Beach, CA 92647; phone: 714.840.8621, hbkosters@verizon.net

Dietmar Kressler, Schloss Odetzhausen, Schlossberg 1-85235, Odetzhausen, Germany; phone: 08134.998 7290

Jerry Lairson, HC 68, Box 970, Ringold, OK 74754; phone: 580.876.3426, bladesmt@brightok.net, www.lairson-custom-knives.net

Ron Lake, 3360 Bendix Ave., Eugene, OR 97401; phone: 541.484.2683

Matthew Lerch, N88 W23462 North Lisbon Rd., Sussex, WI 53089; phone: 262.246.6362, www.lerchcustomknives.com

Neil Lindsay, 323 9th St., Alamosa, CO 81101; phone: 719.588.0716, Linsay@amigo.net

Wolfgang Loerchner, POB 255, Bayfield, Ontario, Canada N0M 1G0; phone: 519.565.2196

R.W. (Bob) Loveless, POB 7836, Riverside, CA 92503; phone: 951.689.7800

Don Lozier, 5394 S.E. 168th Ave., Ocklawaha, FL 32179; phone: 352.625.3576

Dr. Jim Lucie, 4191 E. Fruitport Rd., Fruitport, MI 49415; phone: 231.865.6390, scagel@netonecom.net

Larry and Gail Lunn, 6970 9th Ave. N, St. Petersburg, FL 33710; phone: 727.345.7455

Peter Martin, 28220 N. Lake Dr., Waterford, WI 53185; phone: 262.895.2815, www.petermartinknives.com

Scot Matsuoka, 94-415 Ukalialii Pl., Mililani, HI 96789; phone: 808.625.6658, scottym@hawaii.rr.com

Michael McClure, 803 17th Ave., Menlo Park, CA 94025; phone: 650.323.2596, mikesknives@comcast.net

C.R. Miles Jr., 1541 Porter Crossroad, Lugoff, SC 29078; phone: 803.438.5816

David Mirabile, 1715 Glacier Ave., Juneau, AK 99801; 907.463.3404

Ross Mitsuyuki, 94-1071 Kepakepa St., C-3, Waipahu, HI 96797; phone: 808.671.3335, www.hawaiiangrinds.net

Julius Mojzis, Timravy 6, 985 11 Halic, Slovakia, EU; www.m-art.sk

Dusty Moulton, 135 Hillview Ln., Loudon, TN 37774; phone: 865.408.9779, Dusty@MoultonKnives.com, www.MoultonKnives.com

Jody Muller, 3359 S. 225 RD, Goodson, MO 65663; phone: 417.852.4306, www.mullerforge.com

Bud Nealy, R.R. 1, Box 1439, Stroudsburg, PA 18360; phone: 570.402.1018, budnealy@ptd.net, www.budnealyknifemaker.com

J. Neilson, R.R. 2, Box 16, Wyalusing, PA 18853; phone: 570.746.4944, www.mountainhollow.net

Corbin Newcomb, 628 Woodland, Moberly, MO 65270; phone: 660.263.4639

Don Norris, 8710 N. Hollybrook Ave., Tucson, AZ 85742; phone: 520.744.2494, norrisknives@comcast.net

Stephen Olszewski, 1820 Harkney Hill Rd., Coventry, RI 02816; phone: 401.397.4774, www.olszewskiknives.com, Stephen@olszewskiknives.com

Ken Onion, 47-501 Hui Kelu St., Kaneohe, HI 96744; phone: 808.239.1300, shopjunky@aol.com, www.kenonionknives.com

Fred Ott, 1257 Rancho Durango Rd., Durango, CO 81303; phone: 970.375.9669

Tom Overeynder, 1800 S. Davis Dr., Arlington, TX 76013; phone: 817.277.4812, trovereynderknives@sbcglobal.net, www.overeynderknives.com

Francesco Pachi, Via Pometta, 1, 17046 Sassello (SV), Italy; phone: 019.720086, www.pachi-knives.com

Rik Palm, 10901 Scripps Ranch Blvd., San Diego, CA 92131; phone: 858.530.0407

Bob Patrick, 12642 24a Ave., S. Surrey, British Columbia, Canada V4A 8H9; phone: 604.538.6214, bob@knivesonnet.com

Cliff Parker, 6350 Tulip Dr., Zephyrhills, FL 33544; phone: 813.973.1682

Mike Pellegrin, 107 White St., Troy, IL 62294; phone: 618.667.6777, mikepell3@yahoo.com

Rusty Polk, 5900 Wildwood Dr., Van Buren, AR 72956; phone: 479.410.3661

Flavio Poratelli, via Rossini 14 Bovisio.M, 20030 MI Italy; phone: 0039.0362593805, http://web.tiscalinet.it/flaviopknife, flaviopknife@tiscalinet.it

Vladimir Pulis, CSA 230/95, Kremnica 967 01, Slovak Republic; phone: 00427.45.67.57.214, vpulis@host.sk

J.W. Randall, 11606 Keith Hall Rd., Keithville, LA 71047; phone: 318.925.6480, www.jwrandall-knives.com

Lin Rhea, 413 Grant 291020, Prattsville, AR 72129; phone: 870.699.5095

Ralph Richards, 6413 Beech St., Bauxite, AR 72011; phone: 501.602.5367

George Roberts, Box 31228, 211 Main St., Whitehorse, Yukon Y1A 5P7 Canada; phone: 867.667.7099, bandityukon@canada.com, www.yuk-biz.com/banditblades

Gary Root, 644 E. 14th St., Erie, PA 16503; phone: 814.459.0196

Fred Rowe, Bethel Ridge Forge, 3199 Roberts Rd., Amesville, OH 45711; phone: 866.325.2164, fred.rowe@bethelridgeforge.com, www.bethelridgeforge.com

Michael Ruth, 3101 New Boston Rd., Texarkana, TX 75501; phone: 903.832.7166

Raymond Rybar Jr., 726 W. Lynwood St., Phoenix, AZ 85007; phone: 605.523.0201

Norman Sandow, 20 Redcastle Dr., Dannemora, Howick, Auckland, New Zealand; phone: +64.9.277.0916, sanknife@ezysurf.co.nz

Scott Sawby, 480 Snowberry Ln., Sandpoint, ID 83864; phone: 208.263.4171, scotmar@imbris.net, www.sawbycustomknives.com

Herman Schneider, 14084 Apple Valley Rd., Apple Valley, CA 92307; phone: 760.946.9096

Karl Schroen, 4042 Bones Rd., Sebastopol, CA 95472; phone: 707.823.4057

Paolo Scordia, Via Terralba 143, 00050 Torrimpietra, Roma, Italy; phone: 06.61697231, pands@mail.nexus.it, www.scordiaknives.com

Eugene Shadley, 26315 Norway Dr., Bovey, MN 55709; phone: 218.245.3820, bses@uslink.net

Andy Shinosky, 3117 Meanderwood Dr., Canfield, OH 44406; phone: 330.702.0299, www.shinosky.com

Scott Slobodian, POB 1498, San Andreas, CA 95249; phone: 209.286.1980, www.slobodianswords.com

Jim Sornberger, 25126 Overland Dr., Volcano, CA 95689; phone: 209.295.7819, sierrajs@volcano.net

Bill Sowell, 100 Loraine Forest Ct., Macon, GA 31210; phone: 478.994.9863, billsowell@reynoldscable.net

John Stahl (scrimshaw artist), 2049 Windsor Rd., Baldwin, NY 11510; phone: 516.223.5007, imivory@msn.com, www.imagesinivory.org

Ken Steigerwalt, 507 Savage Hill Rd., Orangeville, PA 17859; phone: 570.683.5156

Jurgen Steinau, Julius-Hart Strasse 44, Berlin 0-1162, Germany; phone: 372.6452512

Murray Sterling, 693 Round Peak Church Rd., Mount Airy, NC 27030; phone: 336.352.5110, sterck@surry.net, www.sterlingcustomknives.com

Russ Sutton, 4900 Cypress Shores Dr., New Bern, NC 28562; phone: 252.637.3963, srsutton@cox.net, www.suttoncustomknives.com

Alberto Symonds, Rambla M.Gandhi 485, Apt. 901, Montevideo, Uruguay; phone: 011.598.2.7103201, albertosymonds@hotmail.com

C. Gray Taylor, 560 Poteat Ln., Fall Branch, TN 37656; phone: 423.348.8304, graysknives@aol.com

Loyd W. Thomsen, Horsehead Creek Knives, HCR 46, Box 19, Oelrichs, SD 57763; phone: 605.535.6162; www.horseheadcreekknives.com.

Colten Tippetts, 4068 W. Miners Farm, Hidden Springs, ID 83714; phone: 208.229.7772

Kathleen Tomey, 146 Buford Pl., Macon, GA 31204; phone: 478.746.8454, Ktomey@tomeycustomknives.com, www.tomeycustomknives.com

Dwight Towell, 2375 Towell Rd., Midvale, ID 83645; phone: 208.355.2419

Leon Treiber, POB 342, Ingram, TX 78025; phone: 830.367.2246

Jean-Jose Tritz, SchopstraBe 23, D-20255 Hamburg, Germany; phone: +49.040.49.78.21

Pete Truncali, 2914 Anatole Ct., Garland, TX 75043; phone: 214.763.7127, ptiii@truncaliknives.com, truncaliknives.com

Reinhard Tschager, Piazza Parrocchia 7, 39100 Bolzano, Italy; phone: 0471.97.06.42, goldtschager@dnet.it

Michael Tyre, 1219 Easy St., Wickenburg, AZ 85390; phone: 928.684.9601, michaeltyre@msn.com

Richard van Dijk, 76 Stepney Ave., RD 2, Harwood, Dunedin, New Zealand; phone: 0064.3.4780401, www.hoihoknives.com

Ricardo Velarde, 7240 N. Greenfield Dr., Park City, UT 84098; phone: 435.940.1378, www.velardeknives.com, ricardovelarde@velardeknives.com

Howard Viele, 88 Lexington Ave., Westwood, NJ 07675; phone: 201.666.2906, h.viele@verizon.net

Donald Vogt, 9007 Hogans Bend, Tampa, FL 33647; phone: 813.973.3245, vogtknives@aol.com

Yasutaka Wada, 2-6-22 Fujinokidai, Nara City, Nara Prefect 631-0044, Japan; phone: 0742.46.0689

Jim Walker, 22 Walker Ln., Morrilton, AR 72110; phone: 501.354.3175, jwalker@mail.cswnet.com

Robert Weinstock, POB 170028, San Francisco, CA 94117; phone: 415.731.5968, weinstock_r@msn.com

Ron Welling, 15446 Lake Ave., Grand Haven, MI 49417; phone: 616.846.2274

Mike Williams, POB 661, Broken Bow, OK 74728; phone: 580.420.3051

Richard Wright, POB 201, Carolina, RI 02812; phone: 401.364.3579, rswswitchblades@hotmail.com, www.richards.wright.com

Joe Zemitis, 14 Currawong Rd., Cardiff Heights NSW 2285 Newcastle, Australia; phone: 0239549907, jjvzem@optusnet.com.au, www.unitedbladeworx.com.au

Mike Zscherny, 1840 Rock Island Dr., Ely, IA 52227; phone: 319.848.3629, Zschernyknives@aol.com

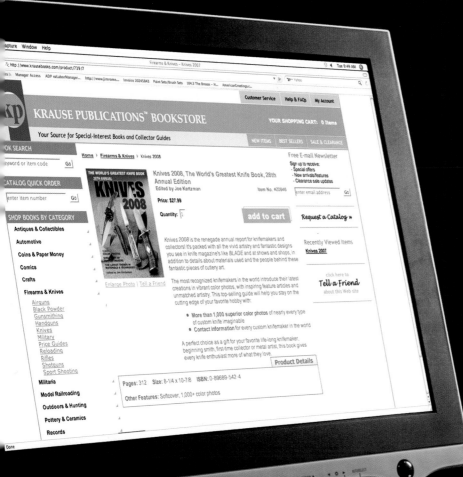